Also By Frank McClain

The Ultimate Job Hunting Guidebook

Winner of **Foreword Reviews'** 2016 *Foreword INDIES Book of the Year Award* and winner of the **Independent Book Publishers Association 2017** *Benjamin Franklin Digital Award*.

The Ultimate Job Hunting Guidebook for Military Veterans

YOU'RE HIRED!

Winner of the **Independent Book Publishers Association 2017** *Benjamin Franklin Digital Award*. Success secrets to phone and in-person job interviews for job seekers and career changers.

IT Questions & Answers For IT Job Interviews, Volume 1
General IT Knowledge, Transmission Lines and Cabling,
Voice over IP (VoIP), Video and Telepresence over IP, Wireless (WiFi)

IT Questions & Answers For IT Job Interviews, Volume 2
IPv4 and IPv6 Addressing, NAT, Layer 2 Switching Concepts,
Layer 3 Routing Concepts

IT Questions & Answers For IT Job Interviews, Volume 3
BGP Routing, EIGRP Routing, OSPF Routing

IT Questions & Answers For IT Job Interviews, Volume 4
Data Center and Virtualization, F5 Networks Load Balancer,
Riverbed WAN Optimization

IT Questions & Answers For IT Job Interviews, Volume 5
Access Lists and Prefix Lists, Tunnels and VPNs, Cisco ASA Firewall

IT Questions & Answers For IT Job Interviews, Volume 6
Service Provider Networks, Quality of Service (QoS),
Troubleshooting Router and Switch Interfaces

THE ULTIMATE JOB INTERVIEW GUIDEBOOK

❖ Conquer Your Fears of Job Interviews

❖ Most Asked Interview Questions & Answers

❖ Complete Job Interview Preparation Guide

❖ Success Secrets to Passing Job Interviews

Frank McClain

Publisher's Note. This publication is designed to provide accurate and authoritative information in regard to the subject matter. It is sold with the understanding that the publisher is not engaged in rendering professional career, legal, financial, psychological or health services. If expert assistance is required, the service of the appropriate professional should be sought.

Edited by Clarence Z. Seacrest

Cover design by Prodesignsx

ISBN 978-1-950059-03-4 (paperback)
ISBN 978-1-950059-04-1 (ebook)
ISBN 978-1-950059-05-8 (ebook)

Dedication

To my Lord and Savior Jesus Christ. Surely Your goodness, mercy and unfailing love have followed me all the days of my life. ~ Psalm 23

Table of Contents

Introduction

Ever wish you could land that new job without having to interview for it? If you are among the 9 out of 10 employed adults who said they fear the job interview, then you're not alone in feeling fearful, intimidated or overwhelmed by the anxiety of having to interview for a job.

According to a *Job Interview Anxiety Survey* conducted by Harris Interactive on behalf of Everest College, the majority of adults (92%) are stressed out about one or more aspects of the job interview process. Of the 1,002 employed adults surveyed by Harris Interactive, 17% said the biggest fear they experienced when seeking their next job was feeling nervous or the jitters about the job interview process; 15% feared being overqualified; another 15% feared being stumped by interview questions; 14% feared being underqualified; and 10% feared they would not be prepared enough to pass their job interview.

The Ultimate Job Interview Guidebook helps you conquer all of these fears so you can approach your next job interview with the assurance and confidence you need to put your fears in the back seat while you remain in control in the driver seat to successfully pass your next job interview and get that job you want.

This guidebook not only shows you how to beat your job interview fears; this book will provide you all the information, preparation and tips to beat out other candidates interviewing for the same job as you. After all, you don't want to just beat your fears; you need to beat out all the competition to land that next job. This guidebook will show you the preparation, information, techniques and tips that all confident job interviewers use to settle their nerves so they can walk into that interview room feeling comfortable and confident as if they own the place.

Whether you have an upcoming phone interview or in-person job interview, ***The Ultimate Job Interview Guidebook*** will show you everything you need to do before, during and after your job interview process to ensure you've covered all the bases. Nothing will be left out.

I realize you could have picked any job interview book to purchase and read. Thank you for choosing my book. I won't waste your money or your time. I have decades of experience in the job hunting and job interview process. I've been on both sides of the job interview table. I've interviewed and successfully passed numerous job interviews; and after I gained years of experience in the workplace, I was the one interviewing candidates for available job openings. So, think of me as your personal job interview coach whose ready to pass on to you the secrets to winning the battle against your interviewing fears and show you what hiring managers are looking for when they interview candidates for jobs.

In *The Ultimate Job Interview Guidebook*, I'll teach you how you can obtain information about the job interview questions before you enter the interview room; and I'll provide you an in-depth look at the most asked questions and how you should answer each question.

Not sure what to wear to your next job interview? No problem. I cover the most current tips on what to wear from top to bottom whether you are male or female; and especially what appearances, colors, accessories, hygiene, scents, hairstyles to avoid that turn off or leave bad impressions on hiring managers and other people interviewing you.

Do you get a case of the sweaty palms, penetrating heartbeat, dry throat, nervous voice, stage fright or haunting fearful thoughts when it's your turn to be interviewed, introduce yourself or answer questions? Let me show you the tried and true methods that will diminish, squash and silence all of those fight-or-flight signs of fear and anxiety, especially the fear of the unknown. I'll walk you through the entire job interview process. This guidebook will explain exactly when and how you should arrive to your job interview; and how to start, continue and finish speaking, listening, sitting and interacting with your interviewers from the time you meet them, during your opening introduction, answering questions, and your closing statements at the end of your job interview. I take the guesswork out of how you should conduct yourself throughout the entire job interview process; and after you apply the principles in this guidebook to your next job interview, you'll have your hiring manager smiling with satisfaction with your job interview performance.

PART ONE

BEFORE THE JOB INTERVIEW

CHAPTER ONE

Job Recruiters Before Job Interviews

Time spent on hiring is time well spent.
Robert Half

How Job Recruiters Can Help You with Job Interviews

One way job-hunters get their foot in the door to job interviews is through external staffing agencies, commonly referred to as "job recruiters", "head hunters" or simply "recruiters". Job recruiting agencies are big business today; and are oftentimes your quickest and easiest path to gaining a job interview. If a staffing agency is the path you plan to take to your next job interview, this section will provide you some valuable information on how you can maximize the use of staffing agencies that will ultimately help you successfully pass your job interview and get hired for the job.

Staffing agency recruiters typically have a lot of information that can help you prepare for your job interview. It's typically easier and quicker to get this information from the job recruiter than researching this information yourself or asking for this type of information during your job interview.

Most job recruiters will be happy to provide you this information or get you this information if they don't have it because, after all, if you don't get hired in your job interview, they don't get paid a commission for submitting you. Therefore, it's in the job recruiter's best interest to provide you this information so that you do well in your job interview.

You will make a better impression on the hiring manager who interviews you if you go into your job interview already knowing some if not all of this information; so always ask the job recruiter to provide you the information in the list below.

- **Name of the company with the job opening:** Having the company name allows you to do some research online at the company's website and through search engines to learn the company's business, history, mission statement, financial status, top brass and department leaders, etc. I'll show you how this information will be useful during the job interview process.

  Some staffing agencies are a bit hesitant to provide you the name of the company with the job opening because they do not want you to bypass them and submit your resume directly to the company's website. That's understandable; recruiters are trying to make a living just like you. If the recruiter does not provide you the name of the company, it is up to you to decide at that point whether or not you want to continue with the recruiter. If the recruiter provides the other information below, I'll oftentimes cut the recruiter some slack and continue working with the recruiter.

- **Location of the company client:** I always ask for the city and, if possible, the address of the company so I can determine if the location of the job is within my desired commute between my home and the employer's worksite. You don't want to waste your time pursuing a job in an area or city that you have absolutely no desire to commute to. Again, some job recruiters may be hesitant to provide you the address. However, by telling the recruiter I simply want to use Google Maps to see how long my commute would be to the work site and what is the best way to get there from my home, the recruiter usually gives me the address.

- **Job description (JD):** The job description (JD) is extremely important because it not only tells you what the responsibilities are in the job opening; it will also identify areas you may need to brush up on or research before the job interview. The JD could be only a few bullet points in length or an entire page depending on the difficulty of the job. If the recruiter does not have the job description, they can get the JD from the employer; so always ask the recruiter to provide you the job description.

- **The industry of the company:** You might work in a career such as administration, IT, warehouse & supply, heating & air conditioning, electrician, medical or lawyer. These types of careers can span multiple industries. You may be inclined to work in some industries but not all of them for one reason or another. Therefore, ask the staffing agency recruiter in what industry does the company belong. You may not want to waste your time interviewing with a company that is in an industry that is not in line with your philosophy, ideology, beliefs or principles.

The following items are additional information you should ask the recruiter to provide you:

- **What is the contract structure?** Is this a full-time company employee position, a contractor position or a contract-to-hire position? If it is a contract position, ask the recruiter how long is the contract?

- **Is this position an exempt or non-exempt position?** Being an **exempt** employee means you are exempt from the Fair Labor Standards Act (FLSA) entitling workers compensation anytime you work beyond the 40-hour workweek. In other words, you are not paid any overtime pay. Those employees who are **non-exempt** from the FLSA regulation concerning overtime will be paid overtime wages for any extra hours worked beyond a 40-hour workweek.

- **Is this position a salaried or hourly position? Salaried workers** are company employees or contractors that are paid a set annual salary, such as $40K, $60K or $100K per year, upon being hired. This set amount paid to the salaried worker each payday does not change regardless of how many hours the person works. Therefore, salary workers typically do not use timesheets. **Hourly workers** are company employees or contractors that are paid by the hour, such as $20, $43.27 or $50 an hour. Unlike the salary worker, the hourly worker must work the full hour to receive the full hourly wage (e.g. $20, $43.27 or $50 an hour). If the worker works less than an hour they will be paid less than their hourly wage for that hour. Therefore, hourly workers typically use timesheets.

- **What work shift is this position?** Is this a straight day job, or is it a swing shift or night shift; or are there weekends involved? If so, that may end your desire to work in that job; or you may have to rethink and readjust your life's schedule for family, children, friends and other activities before pursuing a job interview with this company.

- **How much travel is involved with this position?** Does this job require travel around town or out of state? If so, how often? You can ask the job recruiter this question if it's not stated in the job description.

- **The names of the people that will interview you.** If a staffing agency recruiter is arranging your job interview, they will automatically provide you this information in addition to the address to your interview site once the hiring manager wants to interview you. Most staffing agency recruiters will submit your resume to the hiring manager to get you a job interview. You won't make any contact with the hiring manager yourself until he or she likes what they see in your resume and want to interview you either over the phone or in-person. If you need help with putting together an eye-catching resume that catches the attention of hiring managers, check out my book *The Ultimate Job Hunting*

Guidebook for a thorough explanation and tips on creating the best resume that will help you land that job interview.

Big Brother and Big Sister Job Recruiters

After dealing with many staffing agency recruiters over the years, I've developed a name for some job recruiters that have helped me in my job search and job interview process. I call these particular job recruiters my "big brother" (for a male recruiter) or "big sister" (for a female recruiter). Just as you can talk with your big brother or big sister about things you normally cannot or do not want to talk about with your parents; you can talk to your job recruiter about things that you normally cannot talk about or do not want to talk about with the hiring manager of the "parent" company employer with the job opening.

What things? Things you are better off asking your job recruiter about include your salary (or hourly wage) and benefits for starters. You don't want to ask your hiring manager about these topics. You've probably heard that it is bad form to talk about salary or other company benefits when you are in a job interview. This is true because the hiring manager and other people who are interviewing you are "the parents" so to speak. The hiring manager is part of the company that will make the final decision to hire you. Talking about money and benefits with the hiring manager and other interviewers during your job interview has always been taboo. Engaging in a conversation with them about money or company benefits sheds a negative light on you during the job interview. Why? Because the job interview is always about *"what can you do for the company"*; not *"what the company can do for you"*. I'll go over in more detail what areas you can and cannot talk about during your job interview.

However, you can talk freely to your big brother or big sister—the staffing agency recruiter—about these things. That's one of the reasons why job recruiters are there: to discuss with you all the things that would be considered inappropriate for you to talk about with your hiring manager and other interviewers during your job interview.

And like a big brother or big sister, you can be quite frank and upfront in your conversations—online, in-person or on the phone—with these job recruiters about important compensatory aspects of that available job opportunity, such as salary (or hourly wage) and benefits (medical, dental and vision benefits, 401K, education/certification reimbursement, paid vacation and time off, perks, etc.). They might not have answers to all of your questions about these areas, but at least you know you can ask staffing agency recruiters these types of questions before you attend your job interview with the hiring manager.

If the staffing agency job recruiter hands you off to his or her account manager, you may not hear from that initial recruiter any more at that point; and you will be dealing with that staffing agency's account manager from that point on in trying to get you a job interview with the hiring manager of the company.

Staffing agency recruiters (or account managers) play another important role—as the big brother or big sister I mentioned—after they set up your job interview for you with the hiring manager. Some recruiters will go the extra mile by providing you guidance on how you should prepare for your job interview, such as good grooming tips and proper interview attire; questions about the company or the job you should prepare ahead of time; and how to conduct yourself during your job interview, such as greeting, enthusiasm, posture and taboos. As your job interview coach, I'll provide you all of these same things and much more in this guidebook.

On the day of your job interview, some staffing agency recruiters or account managers who are located in your same local area might meet you at the facility where you will be interviewed; introduce you to one or more of the interviewers; and send you on your way with their vote of confidence—just like a big brother or big sister would do.

If you are happy with the help you received from a staffing agency, it's always a good idea to keep their contact information. Most of us in jobs do not intend to stay in the same workplace forever, so a good staffing agency recruiter becomes a valuable part of your job networking portfolio just as previous colleagues you've work with in the past.

Don't Show All Your Cards to Job Recruiters

When a staffing agency recruiter asks you if you have any job interviews or job offers on the table, don't reveal this information to the recruiter. Recruiters are only asking for this information so they can decide if they should submit your resume to an employer to get you a job interview. If you tell them you do have a job interview lined up or job offer on the table, the recruiter will put off submitting your resume to an employer to get you a job interview. No recruiter wants to submit a resume on a candidate only to have to tell the employer that the candidate was hired by another employer. They would rather pass up on you and submit another job-seeking candidate for the job who they know they have a better chance with. If anything, the recruiter may hold onto your resume; and if none of their other candidates they're working with are not given a job interview or don't pass their interview, they may contact you to see if you were hired in your other job interview. One thing is certain, you'll be the last among their list of job-hunting candidates for potential job interviews.

You don't have to tell the staffing agency recruiter you have a job interview lined up or a job offer on the table if it is for a different job than the one the recruiter is offering you. Put on your poker face and tell the recruiter you've talked with other recruiters but there isn't anything on the table—job interview or job offer. This way, you maintain control of the recruiter; and not the other way around.

CHAPTER TWO

Talking Salary Before, During & After Job Interviews

You have to learn the rules of the game.
And then you have to play better than anyone else.
Albert Einstein

The Golden Rule Concerning Your Salary

The golden rule when it comes to salary negotiation is: **Your highest raise is the salary you negotiate.**

The highest raise you'll most likely ever receive in your current job is the salary you negotiated for that job. Allow me to explain. The time to increase your salary to where you want it to be at is not after you are in that job. The best time to increase your salary to a level you're satisfied with is while you negotiate your salary for that new job whether it's before, during or after the job interview.

Some job seekers will accept whatever salary is offered to them for a particular job, hoping they can increase that salary with raises each year once they're hired. True, you might increase your salary with annual raises (if your company offers raises), but this is not the best way to increase your salary to a higher level.

The quickest way to increase your salary to a higher level you desire for a particular job is to start off by asking for the highest possible salary when you are first hired for that position. This strategy works better than accepting that job at a lower salary; and then expect to receive annual raises to increase your salary to the level you'd like it to be at.

When I was living and working in Europe, I accepted a direct hire position for a large US company in Europe. I accepted the position for a lower salary than I wanted. I took the job hoping after working there each year; the company would reward me with annual raises that would increase my salary to a higher level. What I discovered was that the raises they gave me were only for one or two thousand dollars each year. In my fourth year with this company, I realized my annual salary increases were happening at a much lower and slower rate than I expected for the experience I gained with each new year.

Then I tried something I'm telling you to do. I decided I would try to search for another job and ask for the salary I wanted during salary negotiations. What I discovered during salary negotiations with another company was that this new company was willing to pay me $30,000 more in salary than the salary I was currently making with my previous employer with the raises I received over a 4-year period. Wow!

This is what I mean by saying **the highest raise you'll ever receive is the salary you negotiate**.

I've used this salary-increasing strategy throughout my career for US government and corporate jobs to increase my salary faster and in greater amounts than I could every possibly attain through normal raises that companies give their employees.

Typically, the only other way to get a significant increase in salary within the same company you're working for is by accepting a position change within that company that pays a significantly higher salary. However, that may mean doing a job you may not enjoy, or at least now as much as your previous position within that company. In that case, you're better off finding another job you like that pays you the higher salary you want than to move into another position you don't enjoy within the same company in order to get that higher salary.

Negotiating Salary with Recruiters before Your Job Interview

If you are using a staffing agency to get a job interview with employers, the staffing agency recruiter is the one you want to negotiate your salary and benefits with before your job interview. You don't discuss these things with the hiring manager during your job interview. The hiring manager, and possibly other interviewers, are in your job interview only for the purpose of deciding if they should hire you for their company's job opening.

"But isn't the hiring manager's company the one who is paying me for the job?" you may ask. Yes, but once you negotiate and establish *with the job recruiter* what your desired hourly rate or salary will be, the staffing agency's account manager will check with the hiring manager to get approval of the hourly rate or salary you want. Oftentimes, the staffing agency recruiter already knows the range of salary or hourly rate the hiring manager is willing to pay for the available job opening; therefore, the job recruiter will be able to tell you if your desired compensation fits into the employer's budget for that job. You simply need to discuss (and negotiate) with the job recruiter what salary or hourly rate you're willing to accept for that job.

This process of salary (or hourly wage) negotiation through an intermediary, such as a staffing agency recruiter, is similarly played out among players in professional sports. Pro athletes do not haggle with their team's coaches, management staff or ownership about their millions of dollars they want to be paid. These professional sports players only talk to their "agent" and their agent deals directly with their team ownership. What agents are to these professional athletes when it comes to negotiating money matters with their team ownership, staffing agency recruiters are to us job-seekers in negotiating our salary or hourly wage with companies that have job openings.

Once the staffing agency recruiter agrees to pay your desired compensation and you are asked to be interviewed by the hiring manager; that means the hiring manager agrees to pay you that same amount either directly by the hiring manager's company (if you are a direct hire) or through the staffing agency (if you are a contract hire)—after you pass your job interview and are hired for the job. This may seem like you're putting the cart before the horse—negotiating your salary before you are interviewed and hired for the job—but that's how the job search process works when seeking a job interview through staffing agency recruiters.

After you and the staffing agency recruiter agree to your desired compensation, the recruiter will either continue working with you in getting you a job interview or the recruiter will hand you off to their staffing agency accounting manager who will set up your job interview with the hiring manager who has the job opening.

Why HR Departments or Hiring Managers Ask for Your Salary History

Human Resource (HR) departments and hiring managers ask for your salary history for several reasons, all of which are in the interest of their company, not for your interest or a staffing agency's interest. The reason company HR or hiring managers may want to know your past salary history is because they want to know if your past salaries are higher or lower than what they are willing to pay you. If you provide them your past salary history, especially your most recent salary, they now have a baseline figure on how well your desired salary or hourly rate fits into their budget for their available position they're seeking to fill.

Sharing your salary history before, during or after your job interview can also influence the hiring manager's decision to interview you or HR's desire to hire you for the job. If an HR rep or hiring manager asks you this salary history question before interviewing you, and you answer it, they now have the option of either denying or granting you a job interview based on your desired compensation for the job.

If your previous salaries are below what the company planned to pay for this open position, they can now offer you a lower salary closer to what you made at your last jobs without you knowing they were willing to offer you more money for the job. After all, why should they offer a much higher salary when you were willing to accept a much lower salary in the past? Their reasoning about your salary history may not be what you wanted but that's their thinking anyway. This is playing hard ball. Only thing is, you're the ball. Although your lower salary history increases your chances of being interviewed and hired for the job, you will unknowingly be receiving a much lower salary than what the company was willing to pay for this position.

If your salary history is higher than what they planned to pay for this open position, they can make a quick decision on whether you are still worth interviewing and hiring for the job at the higher salary; or they can pass over you and choose to interview other job-seeking candidates who have a lower salary or lower hourly rate history than you. Your chances of being interviewed for the job or accepted for the position decreases with the number of job-hunting candidates the hiring manager is interviewing with similar qualifications as you who are asking for less money than you. You might be better qualified for the job than those other candidates, but if your desired compensation is much higher than what the hiring manager is willing to pay, the hiring manager may hire the less qualified candidate whose salary expectation is closer to what the hiring manager's company is willing to pay.

However, in some cases, revealing your salary history could also work to your advantage. For example, if you share your salary history showing you made over $70K in past jobs, that tells the hiring manager that they've got to pay you over $70K. If the company's budget allows above a $70K salary for that position, you can more easily request compensation over $70K during salary negotiations with the staffing agency recruiter or directly with the company's HR rep.

Additionally, the HR's or hiring manager's decision to match or beat your past salaries can also be influenced by how well you performed in your job interview with them. Therefore, another goal of this book is to help you perform well in your job interview so that your new company that hires you will also pay you well.

Why Staffing Agencies Ask for Your Salary History

The motive of staffing agency recruiters and account managers for asking you about your previous salaries is slightly different than HR departments or hiring managers of the company with the job opening. The staffing agency could be asking for your salary history on behalf of an hiring manager who requested the staffing agency get that information for them. Staffing agencies can also ask for this information to make their own decisions about submitting job-hunting candidates for job interviews.

Although staffing agencies technically work for the company with the job opening instead of for you, their commission is based on how much salary you will make in your first year with the company. Before recruiters can receive a commission, they know they have to get you into a job interview *and* hired. Therefore, staffing agencies are not only concerned about how your previous salaries compare with what the hiring manager is offering for the job; they have a personal interest in getting you hired so they can get paid a commission. Recruiters know that the higher your first year's salary is in your new job with this company, the larger their commission will be once you're hired.

Staffing agencies typically provide more than one candidate resume to companies looking for people to interview for job openings. If the staffing agency knows the past salaries of several candidates, they can be more selective on which resumes they will submit to companies for job interviews by comparing each candidate's past salaries. If your salary history is much higher than other equally qualified job-seeking candidates, the staffing agency recruiter may once again hold onto your resume and submit other candidate resumes before you that they think have a better chance of getting a job interview based on their lower salary history.

How You Should Respond to the Salary History Question

You have the right to **not** give your salary history to HR, hiring managers or staffing agency recruiters. This is your personal information and you can do with it as you please. Could that result in these people denying you a job opportunity if you refuse to provide past salaries? Absolutely, that's their right too. If this gives you pause for thought, and you choose to provide this information to people asking for it, I respect your decision. Just remember how your past salary information will be used by these organizations if you provide them your salary history.

It really comes down to how much *control* you want over your salary information regardless of the consequences; and how comfortable you are with giving your salary history to these organizations. If you plan to stick by your guns and ask for the salary you want regardless of what you made in the past, then giving your salary information out or keeping that information private simply comes down to your personal preference. You can choose either option depending on how you want to interact with certain HR reps, hiring managers or staffing agencies.

"What if they deny me the job opportunity because I refuse to provide them my salary history?" you ask. So what—there are plenty of other staffing agency recruiters out there trying to contact you for the same or other job opportunities. Most of these other job recruiters won't ask you for your salary history for the same job that another recruiter might be asking you to give.

Personally, I don't bother giving out my salary information to recruiters, HR or hiring managers when they ask for it. I prefer to use the more direct and bullheaded approach when it comes to HR reps, hiring managers or staffing agencies asking me about my past salaries. I tell them I don't give out my salary history. I choose to control my salary information even if it means them refusing to consider me for an interview or the job. I prefer not to give these people that much leverage when it comes to paying me the salary I want. If they don't want to play according to my rules, I'll take my marbles elsewhere and find someone who wants to play by my rules when it comes to my salary history.

I have made one exception to withholding my salary history. Prior to a job interview, I negotiated a salary with a staffing agency that they agreed to pay me should I be hired for the job. Afterward, this staffing agency asked for my salary history. Since they already agreed to pay me what I wanted, I showed them the courtesy of providing them my salary history. There was no way for the staffing agency or the hiring manager to use my salary information as leverage to lower my salary because the staffing agency already agreed to pay me the salary I wanted. After my job interview with the hiring manager, I was hired for the position. I got paid my requested salary and the staffing agency recruiter got their commission. Everyone won in that situation.

CHAPTER THREE

Pre-Screening Before the Job Interview

The sculptor produces the beautiful statue by chipping away such parts of the marble block as are not needed—it is a process of elimination.

Elbert Hubbard

Not all employers use the same job interview process for their job-seeking candidates before selecting which candidate to hire. What many hiring managers typical do is have one in-person interview separately with each job-seeking candidate before they decide who to hire for the available job. However, one hiring manager might pre-screen candidates with written questions (through staffing agency recruiters) first to determine which candidates they will grant a phone interview or in-person interview based on how well they answered the pre-screening questions. Another hiring manager may opt to perform a phone interview first as a screening process to decide which job-seeking candidates they will ask in for an in-person interview. And then there are some hiring managers who choose to have two or three in-person interviews depending on the type or complexity of the position. Usually, the more technical or professional the position is, the greater number of interviews the hiring manager may have before selecting the person for that position.

Prescreening before the Job Interview

As I mentioned, there are some instances where a hiring manager will screen job-hunting candidates with questions before granting them a phone interview or in-person job interview. Hiring managers may use this pre-interview screening process for more technical, professional or senior level positions that require a greater depth of knowledge or experience; or they may require candidates at all levels undergo this prescreening process.

Hiring managers use the prescreening process to filter out job-hunting candidates whose resume caught their eye; but the hiring manager does not want to waste their time interviewing someone who cannot demonstrate the right level of technical or professional knowledge or experience they're looking for in candidates for a specific job opening. Those candidates who answer the prescreening questions well enough to their satisfaction are given either a phone interview or an in-person job interview as the next step, depending on the interviewing process used by the hiring manager. This does not mean you necessarily have to answer every question correctly. I've been granted many in-person job interviews after not answering all of hiring manager's pre-screening questions accurately.

Hiring mangers typically implement this prescreening process in one of two ways:

1. They have the staffing agency recruiter ask you the prescreening questions over the phone.

2. They have the job recruiter email you the questions to complete on your own time.

The good thing about prescreening questions—over the phone or email—from the hiring manager is that these questions give you a sense of the type of questions the hiring manager and other interviewers plan to ask you in the actual phone interview or in-person interview. If you pass the prescreening questions and the hiring manager wants to interview you; pat yourself on the back because this typically means you have the right technical or professional knowledge and/or experience to perform well in the actual job interview.

During one job-hunting occasion, I was seeking work through a staffing agency. The employer sent me six prescreening questions through my staffing agency recruiter. Since I work in the IT profession, most of these questions were accompanied with network drawings having problems I had to decipher and fix before I could properly answer the questions correctly. This is just one example of how prescreening question can be used by employers. Naturally, the employer will tailor these prescreening questions to each person's line of work.

When the Recruiter Asks You the Prescreening Questions

When the staffing agency recruiter asks you prescreening questions on behalf of the hiring manager, the recruiter may start asking you these questions without warning in your first phone conversation with the recruiter. If this happens to you, the first thing you need to realize is the fact that you are actually being prescreened for a future job interview with the hiring manager. Therefore, how you respond to the recruiter is crucial at this point.

This unannounced prescreening could easily catch you off guard because you may want to review some subjects related to the "job description" before being asked these all-important technical or professional questions.

You can do one of two things in response to these unannounced prescreening questions from the job recruiter:

1. Delay the prescreening questions for another day.

2. Start answering the prescreening questions on the spot.

Delay the Prescreening for Another Day

One option is you can tell the staffing agency recruiter that you didn't know they were going to ask you some prescreening questions; and you prefer to have a day or two to go over some of your notes (related to the job description) before you are prescreened with questions. Don't be shy about interrupting the recruiter in the middle of them asking you these prescreening questions to tell them you want to postpone any prescreening questions until later.

If you try to answer these questions immediately over the phone and perform poorly, that will end your chances to be interviewed by the hiring manager and you will not hear from that recruiter again—at least not for that available job opening.

If you tell the job recruiter you want to postpone the questions until you've had a chance to perform a quick review to brush up on some topics, the recruiter will either accept your request and contact you later or try to press you to answer those questions now. Rarely will the recruiter pass over you and move on to another candidate when you ask to postpone the prescreening questions. Once the recruiter has contacted you, it means the computerized Applicant Tracking System (ATS) the recruiter used to find you thinks your resume is a good fit for the job opening. Therefore, the recruiter is not going to walk away from you so easily. That would be like throwing money away, or in job recruiter terms, throwing their commission away.

Most companies, especially large companies and staffing agencies, use a computerized ATS system to search, collect, filter and sort, organize, process, store and manage thousands of online resumes and candidate information from different Internet job search and social media websites. This makes it quicker and easier for staffing agency recruiters and human resource (HR) departments of companies reviewing resumes to locate, select, track and communicate with the best candidates or the top 10 candidates that meet the requirements for job openings they are trying to fill.

You are only going to have one shot at these prescreening questions. Instead of worrying about what the job recruiter might think of you asking them to wait a day or two for you to answer those prescreening questions, you should be focused more on passing these questions well enough so that you will get an invitation from the hiring manager for a phone interview or in-person job interview. So, if you need to postpone the prescreening questions a couple of days to brush up on some of the items that are listed in the job description, tell the job recruiter to hold off on the questions a day or two.

If you haven't even seen the job description from the job recruiter yet, ask the recruiter to send you a copy of the job description first before answering the prescreening questions. No doubt, the prescreening questions will cover areas listed in the job description.

Start Answering the Prescreening Questions on the Spot

The second option is you can accept this unexpected challenge on the spot and start answering these prescreening questions off-the-cuff based on your experience, comfort level and confidence in answering these types of questions.

I've responded with both of these options at different times in the past when being prescreened over the phone by staffing agency recruiters who unexpectedly started asking me job-related questions. It just depends on how well prepared you are at the time for these prescreening questions from job recruiters.

When the Recruiter Emails You the Prescreening Questions

In other instances, the staffing agency recruiter or account manager might email you the hiring manager's prescreening questions. When a hiring manager wants to screen candidates this way, the good news is that it is like taking an open book test in school. You can take your time answering these questions, reading or researching information online or in your own books or notes to answer the questions. There's typically no time limit set to complete these questions, but you should complete them as expeditiously as possible if you want to be considered for an interview for this job.

When you are done answering the questions, you simply email your answers back to the staffing agent who will forward your answers to the hiring manager for review. If the hiring manager is pleased with your answers and wants to interview you, the recruiter will let you know and ask you when the best day and time is for you to be interviewed by the hiring manager.

Sometimes, it may take over a week before the recruiter provides you feedback from the hiring manager because someone on the interview team who is reviewing your answers may be preoccupied with other work-related priorities or the hiring manager may be on a business or personal trip. If you do not hear back from the recruiter after 1–2 weeks, you should either call or email the recruiter for feedback.

CHAPTER FOUR

The Phone Interview

The most valuable of all talents is that of never using two words when one will do.
Thomas Jefferson

The phone interview we are discussing in this section is not the phone conversations you will have with a staffing agency recruiter or account manager about a job opportunity. This phone interview is the "job interview" you have with the hiring manager and possibly other interviewers over the phone.

After the staffing agency or company HR department forwards your resume over to the hiring manager, it is the hiring manager who makes the final decision if he or she will interview you by either phone or in-person.

Phone interviews are an elimination process

The phone interview is oftentimes a vetting and elimination process that hiring managers use to determine which job-hunting candidates they want to bring in for an in-person job interview. The main difference between the phone interview and the pre-screening questions I just covered is that the phone interview will involve more questions from the hiring manager and other interviewers that are on the phone with you.

Make no mistake about it: the phone interview is equally important as an in-person job interview because you only get one shot at the phone interview just as with most in-person interviews.

Your ultimate goal in the phone interview is to impress the hiring manager and other interviewers enough to make them want to invite you in for an in-person job interview. If you do not impress your interviewers over the phone, they will pass over you and that will be the end of any further chances you have of being interviewed in-person for that available job.

If you do not pass your phone interview, it will do you no good to try to resubmit your resume to the same hiring manager again through another recruiting agency or through the company's website. The hiring manager and the rest of the interviewing team have already seen your resume; so they will know it is you again; and they will simply toss your resume in the trash.

If you pass your phone interview, you will be notified by your staffing agency recruiter or account manager that the hiring manager liked you and wants you to come in for an in-person job interview. Passing the phone interview does not necessarily mean you will be hired for the job. However, it does mean you now stand a better chance of being hired because you impressed the hiring manager and other interviewers enough during this first elimination round (the phone interview) to make them want to interview you in person. You should accept this next invitation from the hiring manager as a big boost of confidence that the interviewers liked what they heard from you over the phone from both a technical/professional fit and cultural fit standpoint. I'll explain the "technical/professional fit" and "cultural fit" in detail later.

Stay on top of your game because you are still competing against other job-seeking candidates for this job that the hiring manager has already interviewed before you or plans to interview after you.

Although it is only a phone interview, you should still follow all the applicable guidelines I will point out in the *Before the Interview* and *During the Interview* chapters. Don't wait until after a successful phone interview to learn and follow these tips, advice and procedures outlined in these chapters on job interview preparation.

How Phone Interviews Benefit the Hiring Manager

Phone interview conference calls allow the hiring manager and perhaps other interviewers to either gather together in their company conference room or sit at their separate desks at work while they interview you. A phone interview conference call also allows interviewers who may be working in different locations across the country to interview you along with the interviewers in your local area.

If the hiring manager and other interviewers gather together in their private conference room at work to interview you over the phone, they will receive your call over the open speaker phone so everyone in the room can hear you speak.

If the hiring manager and other interviewers are at their individual desks while interviewing you over the phone, each of them typically wear their phone headsets to hear you speak and to ask you questions. This way, everyone in the office does not hear you being interviewed for the job opening.

How Phone Interviews Benefit You

Phone interviews can also be advantageous to you as the job-hunter as well. A phone interview can be a better option than an in-person interview during times when you are job-hunting while still employed in another job. If you are not working, a phone interview also means you don't have to get dressed up or drive to the job interview location.

I've interviewed for jobs while employed by stepping outside of my workplace and going to the privacy of my car to interview for jobs. During a break at work, I've also gotten in my car; drove to a quiet secluded location; and then called in for a phone interview.

When I'm not working, I've interviewed for many jobs via phone at home. I oftentimes preferred the phone interview over the in-person interview because it meant I didn't have to get dressed up and drive to another location for the job interview.

A phone interview also provides you the unique advantage of having your computer, resume and notes in front of you while talking to your interviewers over the phone; something I always do when I'm being interviewed over the phone at home.

If you will be interviewed over the phone, pick a location where you can be alone that is quiet and free from distraction. The optimum location for you may be in a room in your home, in your car or some other private area.

How to Call in for a Phone Interview

If the hiring manager wants to interview you by phone, the staffing agency recruiter or account manager will provide you the conference call phone number and a passcode number to call on the day and time of your scheduled job interview. The conference call phone recording will tell you when to use the passcode number after you've called in on your phone.

Just as it is wise to arrive early for an in-person job interview, you should call the hiring manager's number **2–5 minutes** before your scheduled phone interview time. Calling in late for a phone interview makes just as bad an impression as arriving late to an in-person job interview. It reflects poorly on your ability to plan ahead and perform tasks in a punctual manner.

Once you are on the conference call, the interviewer's phone system will tell you how many people are currently on the conference call. Once you are connected to the conference call, you should introduce yourself by stating your full name, such as *"Frank McClain is on the line"*, so that if one of the interviewers are already on the line, they'll know you have arrived for your scheduled phone interview.

If you are the first person on the conference call, wait patiently for someone to arrive. Once you hear someone on the line, again state your full name to let them know you, the job candidate, are on the line for your job interview. One of the interviewers on the conference call will let you know if they are still waiting for other interviewers to call in.

Once all the interviewers have called in to the conference call, the hiring manager or team lead will start things off with introductions just as in an in-person job interview; and everything will continue through to the end of your job interview as it normally would during an in-person job interview. In these next chapters, I'll go over this entire job interview process in great detail, so don't worry.

CHAPTER FIVE

Job Interview Preparation and Tips

We are what we repeatedly do. Excellence then is not an act, but a habit.
Aristotle

Now you have an appointment for a job interview in the next couple of days—***Congratulations***! However, this is not the time to sit back and wait until your interview day arrives. There's still more work to be done— it's called **pre-interview preparation**.

As with many things in life, preparation is one of the keys to success. Without it, all plans, great and small, can fail. No matter how educated, knowledgeable, gifted, talented, smart, experienced or resourceful you are—***you need preparation***. This is also true when it comes to your next job interview.

You've uploaded your resume on Internet job search websites and talked with job recruiters. You've done your job search and found a job at a company you'd like to work at. You've negotiated your salary with a staffing agency recruiter and they submitted your resume to the hiring manager; or you submitted your resume yourself to a company you'd like to work at. Now the hiring manager would like to interview you for the job.

Everything you've done up to this point was for that job interview, but your effort doesn't end here. Depending on the number of job-seeking candidates who want that same job, you may be in competition with other people during the job interview process; and as with many job openings, only one person may be getting hired for that job. So now is not the time to rest on your laurels until the day your job interview arrives.

I realize for some of you, the job interview is the most difficult part because you're among the majority of job seekers that gets nervous about job interviews. I wrote this book especially for you. I'm going to share with you the preparation needed to reduce and eliminate your fears and successfully pass your job interview.

Carli Lloyd is the professional midfielder soccer player and co-captain of the US women's national soccer team; scoring the famous three goal hat trick within 16 minutes in that final match against Japan that won the 2015 FIFA Women's World Cup championship among 23 other international teams. She is also a two-time Olympic gold medalist and the 2015 FIFA Player of the Year. When it comes to preparation, Lloyd said, *"The harder you work and the more prepared you are for something, you're going to be able to persevere through anything."*

The same is true when it comes to preparing for your job interview.

Start with a Thank You

If you had a staffing agency help you get that job interview, your first order of business should be to thank your staffing agency recruiter or account manager for setting up your interview with the hiring manager. In the excitement of being notified that the hiring manager wants to interview you, don't forget to take the time to show you're a classy person by thanking the staffing agent for their part in this all-important job interview process. Show the staffing agent you are a classy professional by expressing your appreciation for their efforts thus far. This can be done by a simple thank you to the staffing agency recruiter (or account manager) over the phone after they giving you the good news about your upcoming job interview or you can send a thank you email or text to the recruiter if you've been communicating online.

First Impressions Are Lasting Impressions

The job interview is all about making a good impression on the hiring manager and other interviewers that may be in your job interview. It starts with the first impression you make upon your arrival at the job interview and continues throughout your interview to your last impression you make at the end of your job interview.

The old saying *first impressions are lasting impressions* is perhaps never more impactful in your adult life than with job interviews. The first impression you display at your job interview could mean the difference between you paying off the mortgage on a home or losing a home; paying off your debt or watching the bills pile up; having something or losing something; only dreaming it or actually living it; starting over or going under—**impactful**. Only you know just how impactful your next job interview is going to be to you, your loved ones and your place and status in life.

The job interview as a whole is the first and perhaps only opportunity you will have to make a good enough impression on those interviewing you to influence them to either hire you for the job or invite you back for a second interview if their interview process requires more than one job interview before hiring someone for the job.

I'm going to help you in your preparation to make a great impression on your hiring manager and any other interviewers so you seal the deal in being hired for that job. That's what this chapter is about.

Give Yourself Time to Prepare for the Job Interview

With preparation comes familiarity and a renewed sense of normalcy in the thing prepared that produces better results, greater confidence and comfortability when you move from preparation to application. Therefore, you want to be as prepared as you possibly can before you go into the job interview so that what you are seeing, thinking, feeling and experiencing during the job interview feels as familiar, normal and comfortable as possible to you. This will make you feel more confident and comfortable throughout the entire job interview process. As with all things however, preparation takes time. Don't worry; I purposely kept this book short enough to allow you time to go over this material.

In this chapter, we're going to take the time to ensure you have all the information you need before your upcoming job interview, such as what you should research ahead of time; how to make a good impression with your hiring manager and other interviewers; how you should dress for success; what questions might be asked; and what you should do and say at the start, during and at the end of your job interview. This information will help you cover all the important key areas that will give you the greatest chances for success in your next job interview.

In the next chapter, I'll go over all the details you need to know about the dynamics of job interviews while you are actually in the room with the hiring manager and other interviewers; how to conduct yourself and interact with those interviewers to make the best impression; what things you should focus on and talk about and what things to avoid; and what the hiring manager and other interviewers are looking for in you and in your answers.

I've been down this road many times and have learned what it takes to be prepared for and successfully pass many job interviews. I've also learned the secrets to removing all fears of the job interview. I'm completely confident and comfortable every time I go into a job interview because I've learned the secrets to preparing well for job interviews. Did I answer every one of their questions in my job interviews? Most of the time, no, but I learned how to make a good impression that influenced the hiring manager to hire me. Now I'm going to show you how to do the same thing in these next two chapters.

An Overview of Job Interview Preparation

The following list is the key areas you should focus on when preparing for your upcoming job interview. I'll break down each of these key areas in great detail and show you what you need to know about each area to ensure you're completely prepared for your next job interview.

- Scheduling the job interview

- Appearance and attire for job interviews

- Research the company

- The hiring manager or other interviewers

- Research the job description

- Your resume for the job interview

- Certifications and experience over education in job interviews

- Arrival at your job interview

- Introductions in your job interview

- Job interview questions and answers

- Cultural fit questions and answers

- Questions to ask the interviewers and closing the job interview

- Role-playing job interviews

Scheduling the Job Interview

After the staffing agency recruiter or account manager informs you that the hiring manager wants to interview you, they will ask you when you can come in for a job interview (if it is an in-person interview) or when can you be interviewed over the phone. If you are prepared and ready to interview, give them a day and timeframe that works best for your schedule. You should provide a specific timeframe that fits into your work schedule (if you are employed) or your personal schedule (if you are not employed). If the day and time is not a factor for you, you can tell the staffing agency or HR department that you will accept whatever time the hiring manager has available to interview you.

If you're not prepared for the job interview, you should ask to be interviewed in 2–3 days. This will allow you sufficient time for the preparation outlined in this book for your job interview.

Do not ask for a week or more before you are ready to interview. Waiting this long will make the hiring manager think you are either not interested in the job or you are interviewing for other jobs; both of which will reflect poorly on you.

Sometimes the hiring manager is under a tight interview schedule because of the number of candidates they are interviewing for the same job or due to their company's work priorities at the time. In this case, the hiring manager may provide you several dates and times you can choose from; and you simply have to pick one of those dates and times as your job interview appointment.

Once you've given the staffing agency recruiter or account manager your desired interview date and time, the staffing agency will forward your requested interview appointment to the hiring manager. If there are any conflicts in schedules, the staffing agency will let you know.

If all parties can make it to your desired job interview appointment, the staffing agency will send you a confirmation email. This email usually includes the names of some or all of your interviewers; the address of the interview location (if it is an in-person interview) or the phone number to call (if it is a phone interview); and the scheduled date and time all parties have agreed to be present for your job interview.

Appearance and Attire for Job Interviews

What better way to start off our discussion about first impressions than with appearance and attire; but first a reality check—the phone interview.

Many hiring managers prefer to have their first interview with you over the phone instead of in person. If this is the case for you, the staffing agent will let you know, and you will not have to concern yourself with this section on *"Appearance and Attire for Job Interviews"*.

However, if the hiring manager likes how you answered their questions over the phone, the hiring manager is going to either hire you for the job (hurray!) or they are going to ask you to come in for a second "in-person" interview (hurray!). If the latter is true and the hiring manager wants you to come in for an in-person job interview; then that's when this section on appearance and attire will matter to you most.

How Your Appearance and Attire Makes an Impression

Whether you are asked to come in for an in-person job interview once, twice or three times, you should always dress as professional in your second and third interviews as you would for the first. If you are dressed appropriately, this will start your job interview off on the right foot. What you are wearing is the first thing the hiring manager and other interviewers will notice about you when you arrive for your job interview. Your appearance will form their first of many first impressions of you within seconds of your first meeting. If you are dressed unprofessionally or inappropriately, this will impact the hiring manager's decision in hiring you.

The staffing agency recruiter or account manager who submitted your resume and got you the job interview may also be meeting you for the first time at the hiring manager's facility. You want to dress well so they know you know how to dress the part for your all-important job interview.

If you've been to a lot of job interviews as I have, it's not long before you notice that every time you show up for the job interview looking your best in your professional-looking suit and tie, the interviewers are always wearing the typical casual dress people normally wear to work. If you work in an industry that typically dresses casual, you're usually met by interviewers wearing khaki pants; a worn buttonless short sleeve shirt or casual button-down long sleeve shirt with the tails hanging out; and shoes that look a bit worse for the wear.

If you feel a bit overdressed sitting there in that room in your suit and tie or business dress while they all get to wear casuals; just remember one thing about your job interview: the job interview is all about *you*, not the interviewers. They've all been through what you're going through in the job interview process and they got the job. They expect you to show up dressed as professionally as they did when they had to interview for their jobs; not in casual wear that you see them dressed in at your job interview.

They were working that morning long before you arrived for your scheduled job interview; and they most likely have to keep working long after you leave. In other words, they earned the right to wear those casuals during your job interview. What they're doing now, sitting across from you in their casuals, is taking time out of their busy day to focus solely on you. You're the one looking for the job, not them. It's all about you, so enjoy the attention they're giving you despite their busy work schedule and casual appearance.

Something else you may not be aware of is that when all of those interviewers wearing casuals want to get promoted or move to a different position within that company, they have to get all dressed again just like you and go through a similar job interview process as you. I've seen that happen many times in companies where I've worked. In other words, those interviewers in your job interview wearing casuals don't necessarily get a free pass when they're seeking a new position within that company in the future. They have to go through what you're going through in your job interview all over again; although there may be special instances where they don't have to be interviewed for another position within that company.

Your hiring manager and other interviewers will appreciate the fact that you took your job interview seriously enough to dress appropriately for the occasion, just like they had to when they were interviewed for their job in that company. Your appropriate response in dressing well for this job opportunity is another good first impression, even though your interviewers appear to be underdressed for the occasion. After you are hired, you'll be back to wearing the same casuals alongside the rest of them.

How to Dress for Visits to Staffing Agencies

When the staffing agency is in your local area, the job recruiter may ask you to come in to their office first before they arrange a job interview between you and the hiring manager. Typically, you wouldn't wear a suit and tie for these recruiter meet-and-greet sessions as you would for a job interview with the hiring manager. However, this visit at the recruiter's office is a different type of interview—it is a **pre-screening interview**.

The staffing agency recruiter oftentimes asks you to come to their office because they want to see your personal appearance and how you present and conduct yourself. From the time you enter the staffing agency's door and shake the recruiter's hand until you say your goodbyes in departing; the job recruiter will be evaluating your appearance and their own comfort level in introducing you to potential employers.

Based on how you look and act in this introductory meeting, the recruiter will make their final decision on whether they should submit your resume to the employer *or not*. Therefore, dress appropriately in a business casual outfit to these meetings with job recruiters. You can use some of the guidelines I provide in this section to pick out certain colors and materials in your outfit that are just as appropriate for the recruiter meeting as they are for your actual job interview with the hiring manager.

Most staffing agency recruiters expect you to wear something business casual. That usually means wearing something that falls between suit and tie (for men)/business outfit (for women) and jeans. For example, slacks or khaki pants with a neat open collar shirt (no tie), neatly groomed and clean shoes (no tennis shoes or sandals). If I decide to visit the staffing agency recruiter at their office, I'll ask the recruiter if they'd like me to come in dressed in business casual. They usually agree.

How to Dress for Seasonal or Holiday Jobs

A great way to supplement your income or have extra spending money is finding temporary jobs during the summer, winter or holidays.

Contrary to the information about the slowdown in hiring across most industries during November and December, these winter months also see a hiring increase in certain industries such as retail stores between Thanksgiving and Christmas. Retailers in clothing, jewelry, sporting goods, electronics and holiday gifts increase their workforce during the higher volume sales months of November and December. Included in this list are restaurants, party suppliers, holiday decoration centrals, and winter attractions such as ski resorts. Other markets that seek out extra help during the certain holidays are post offices and other warehouse, fulfillment center, shipping and transportation companies, and online distributers because consumer spending has moved from brick-and-mortar toward click-and-order.

Many companies start preparing for this holiday rush by hiring more people for temporary work (part-time and full-time) as early as August or September for the final two months of the year. Most of these jobs are temporary because companies only need the extra personnel to handle the increase of customers during the holidays. Once the customer traffic and buying dies down, so do these positions.

Although these jobs are only temporary, it gives many people an opportunity to gain experience and skills; network with people in the workforce; build their resume; and possibly open the door to a permanent position with the company. Don't forget the discounts you'll receive with many retail companies while working there temporarily.

Even though it may be only a seasonal or holiday job at Walmart, JCPenny, Target, Amazon or another retailer or shipping company; you should always dress appropriately when inquiring about an available seasonal position at these businesses. Rules about first impressions apply when hiring managers at retail stores and shipping companies meet you for the first time too. It doesn't matter if you're applying for a job at Home Depot and everyone there wears jeans. You're not one of their employees dressed for work. You're a person on the outside looking for a job on the inside. Hiring managers, including Home Depot hiring managers, expect you to dress neatly when you ask for a job application to work at their store. It may be the deciding factor on whether they provide you a job application or tell you they have no openings.

When inquiring about job openings at Walmart, JCPenny, UPS or other businesses, a business suit for men or a business outfit for women is not required. However, you should be dressed neatly in business-casual attire, such as conservative neat slacks, a collared shirt (a tie is appropriate for clothing stores and other retailers where workers wear ties) and polished shoes for men; and conservative neat slacks or dress, blouse and shoes for women.

Prepare Your Attire Ahead of Time for the Job Interview

Once you have an appointment for an in-person job interview, one of the first things you should do is go over your attire you plan to wear to the job interview. This is important because you may discover your business suit, outfit, skirt, shirt, blouse or shoes need cleaning, mending or replacing.

If you're in a time crunch, the cleaners can press and clean your clothes faster than their normal service but you'll have to pay a little extra for that. However, this still may take a day or two, hopefully in time before your job interview.

Mending your clothes or shopping for something new also takes time. You don't want to be scrambling to accomplish these things the day of your interview when you're trying everything on. If you need to buy a business suit or business outfit, ask the salesperson at the clothing store for advice in picking out a conservative business suit or business outfit for a job interview. They'll be able to point you in the right direction— part of their job is to help make you look good for the right occasion.

If your budget allows, do yourself a favor and have a clean and pressed outfit set aside and ready for any job interview. Cover it in a plastic garment bag and hang it in your closet to keep it protected and free of lint or dust. You can purchase garment bags for as low as $6–$12 online or at your local shopping center.

Although I have several suits, I always have one suit with a clean white shirt that I only use for job interviews, covered in a garment bag hanging in my closet. The day before my job interview, I pull my suit out of the garment bag; pick out a tie, belt, socks and shoes; and try everything on as a final pre-check to make sure all of my clothing is ready to wear the following day for my job interview.

Conservative is king

When it comes to your selection and fashion of outfits, conservative is king for job interviews. You are attending a business function when you go to a job interview; not a night out on the town or a party. Therefore, your choice of colors, material, fashion and fit in your attire should reflect this business event.

There may also be organizations in your local area that provide assistance to job-seekers with their job interview attire. For example, in my city of Denver, Colorado, there is the *Dress For Success Denver* organization that helps provide women with a network of support, professional attire and development tools to give them the greatest chance to succeed and thrive in job interviews and the workplace.

I also provide you a list of conservative dress items for both men and women who are preparing for their next job interview. These colors, materials, fashion and fit are tried and true conservative choices used in every industry for job interviews. You can't go wrong with these guidelines.

Recommendations for Men's Appearance and Attire for an Upcoming Job Interview:

- **Suit:** Well-fitting, clean and pressed two-piece single-buttoned business suit with matching jacket and pants made of natural fibers such as wool; in conservative colors, such as dark navy blue or charcoal (dark gray). Do not mix colors or materials in the jacket and pants. No missing buttons, lint or smell of smoke.

- **Shirt:** Clean, pressed (or ironed yourself) long-sleeved button-down shirt in white or light blue solid color or conservative stripes. No stains around the collar or missing buttons. [**For recruiter meetings:** other conservative colors are acceptable.]

- **Tie:** Conservatively designed silk tie that coordinates with your suit color. Avoid bow ties, flashy ties meant for parties or night clubs, and fashion extremes such as character ties.

- **Shoes:** Cleaned and polished conservative shoes in black, dark brown or cordovan (burgundy) matching the color of your belt. Shoes can be lace-up or slip-on business shoes.

- **Belt:** Conservative belt in black, dark brown or cordovan (burgundy) matching the color of your shoes.

- **Socks:** Conservative dark single-colored socks that coordinates with, and is equal to or darker than, your pants color. The socks color should not be lighter in color than your pants. Avoid multi-colored socks with different patterns.

- **Hair and Facial:** Hair should be clean, well-kept and cut if needed. Avoid extreme or unnatural-looking hair colors during the interview. Facial hair, such as beards or mustaches, should be neatly trimmed or cleanly shaven (no stubble look). This doesn't mean you can't ever grow the stubble look or a full beard; you should wait until after you are hired to do that (contractors and employees do this all the time). Clip visible nose hairs. You can purchase an electric nose clipper at your local shopping center. No hats.

- **Mouth:** Brush your teeth and don't eat after you have brushed; otherwise, brush your teeth again. Have fresh breath (breath mints or sprays can help in this area). Don't smoke right before your interview. No gum, candy or other objects in your mouth during the interview.

- **Hands:** Clean hands; fingernails cleaned and trimmed to short length. No gloves.

- **Tattoos:** Conceal visible tattoos if possible.

- **Fragrance:** Little to no fragrance, such as cologne, after shave lotion or hair scents. Wear deodorant. Avoid smoking while in your suit to prevent the smell of smoke when in the interview room.

- **Watch or jewelry:** Conservative, nice watch (if you choose to wear one). A finger ring is acceptable, such as wedding, engagement or school rings. Other than wedding and engagement rings, the ring should be conservative, not flashy. Avoid wearing stackable rings, midi rings or multiple rings on several fingers. Avoid necklaces, bracelets and leather wraps. Avoid jewelry with political, religious or designs or insignia representing a movement or lobby. No visible body piercings.

- **Accessories:** Clean and conservative notebook, portfolio or slim briefcase (for holding unfolded resumes, notepad and writing pen). The portfolio or briefcase should coordinate with the color of your shoes. No pictures promoting your favorite sports team, movie or other images on the notebook or carrying device. No backpacks or other book bags. The interviewers normally have their own copy of your resume they received from the recruiter; therefore, a simple small notebook or portfolio should do if you need to bring these things. No need to bring documents showing your previous work unless you are told to do so before the interview.

Recommendations for Women's Appearance and Attire for an Upcoming Job Interview:

- **Suit, Dress or Skirt:** Well-fitting, clean and pressed pant suit, skirted suit or, as a last choice, a dress and blouse under a blazer or jacket. Pant suit, skirted suit or dress should be made of natural fibers such as wool or wool blend; in conservative colors, such as dark navy blue or charcoal (dark gray). Other less used but acceptable colors is neutral colors, such as beige, brown or possibly dark red or burgundy. Jacket can be 1 or 2-button. Do not mix colors or materials in the jacket/blazer and pants. If using a jacket over a dress, ensure colors match well with each other. No missing buttons, lint or smell of smoke. Dress or skirt should be of moderate length, not above the knee.

- **Blouse:** Clean, pressed (or ironed yourself) long sleeve blouse made of cotton or silk in white or another light color such as pastel. [For recruiter meetings: other conservative colors are acceptable.] Avoid low cut or sheer blouses. No stains around the collar or missing buttons. No camisole tops.

- **Hosiery:** Clean in neutral color such as tan or sheer black. Avoid white nylons. No runs or holes.

- **Shoes:** Cleaned and polished, conservative, moderate height heels or pumps (1–1 ½ inch) or flats in black, dark brown or cordovan (burgundy) matching the color of your belt.

- **Belt:** If used, should be conservative in black, dark brown or cordovan (burgundy) matching the color of your shoes.

- **Hair and Facial:** Hair should be clean, conservative and worn in a comfortable fashion, yet a polished, stylish look that's free of frizz and flyaways. Wrapped sleek-looking ponytail or bun, top not or French twist are acceptable. Avoid hair styles that cover your face or eyes during the interview. Avoid extreme or unnatural-looking hair colors during the interview. Makeup should accentuate your facial features and make you feel confident and comfortable without overdoing it or going to extremes, such as in a runway fashion show. Avoid using eyeshadow, smoky eye, double wing, cut crease or cat's eye makeup to an interview (save that look for your night out on the town). Clip visible nose hairs. You can purchase an electric nose clipper at your local shopping center. No hats.

- **Mouth:** Brush your teeth and don't eat after you have brushed; otherwise, brush your teeth again. Have fresh breath (breath mints or sprays can help in this area). Don't smoke right before your interview. No gum, candy or other objects in your mouth during the interview.

- **Hands:** Clean hands with fingernails cleaned, unchipped and well-manicured. Nail polish, if used, should be a conservative neutral shade, such as sheer, taupe, beige, mild pink or clear nail polish. Avoid nail art, sparkles, neons and stripes nail polish for the interview. No gloves.

- **Tattoos:** Conceal visible tattoos if possible.

- **Fragrance:** Little to no fragrance, such as perfume, lotions or moisturizers, creams, hair spray or scents. Wear deodorant. Avoid smoking while in your outfit to prevent the smell of smoke when in the interview room.

- **Watch or jewelry:** Conservative, nice watch (if you choose to wear one). Small, simple, conservative earrings or studs in gold, silver, pearl or diamond are acceptable. Avoid big hoops, dangling or whimsical motif earrings. A finger ring is acceptable, such as wedding, engagement or school rings. Other than wedding and engagement rings, the ring should be conservative, not flashy. Avoid wearing stackable rings, midi rings or multiple rings on several fingers. A conservative, thin necklace in gold, silver, pearl, or small pendant are acceptable. Avoid layered or large necklaces and large pendants. Avoid bracelets, bangles and leather wraps. Avoid jewelry with political, religious or designs or insignia representing a movement or lobby. No visible body piercings.

- **Accessories:** Clean, conservative, professional-looking notebook, portfolio or slim briefcase (for holding unfolded resumes, notepad and writing pen). The portfolio or briefcase should coordinate with the color of your shoes. Avoid bringing a purse. No pictures promoting your favorite sports team, movie or other images on the notebook or carrying device. No backpacks or other book bags. The interviewers normally have their own copy of your resume they received from the recruiter; therefore, a simple small notebook or portfolio should do if you need to bring these things. No need to bring documents showing your previous work unless you are told to do so before the interview.

Research the Company

In Chapter One about obtaining information from staffing agency recruiters, I covered the importance of getting the name of the company where the recruiter will submit your resume, as well as getting the company address. Once you know the name of the company, you can perform a thorough online search of the company's website in addition to other information about the company on Internet search engines, such as DuckDuckGo, Yahoo!, Bing or Google; or on social media sites, such as Facebook or LinkedIn.

Now that you have that company information, it's time to use that information to your advantage in preparation for your job interview. Review the following information on the company's website, social media and other online sites in preparation for your job interview with that company:

- **Company's purpose and mission statement:** Familiarize yourself with what that company does. If the company's home page does not provide this information, look in the "*About Us*", "*Who We Are*" or "*What We Do*" sections of the company website.

   During the introductions in your job interview, the hiring manager will oftentimes tell you about their company first, as well as how the team you'll be on (once you are hired) fit into the company picture. However, you should always have a good understanding of the company's purpose, mission and goals before you go into the job interview. This will make you feel more confident and comfortable about the company's mission; and will help confirm what the hiring manager says about the company.

- **Company history and latest news:** Read about when, where and how the company was created; growth (in personnel, locations, acquisitions and annual revenue) over the years; and most recent news. This company information is usually found in the *"About Us"*, *"Who We Are"* or *"News & Events"* sections of the company website.

  At the end of your job interview when it's your turn to ask the hiring manager any questions you may have or provide closing comments, this is a good time to share what you know about the company in your closing conversation. Share your knowledge of important recent news about the company or about other states where this company operates to show the hiring manager your research and interest in their company. This will make another good impression on the hiring manager because it shows you were interested enough in their company to research about it.

  When I'm researching the company, I usually jot down some notes about the company on a piece of paper that I bring with me to the job interview. At the end of the job interview, when they ask me if I have any questions, I'll pull out and reference these notes during my closing comments.

- **Company posts and reviews:** There are other places you can learn about a company besides the company's own website. If you type in the company's name using an online search engine, you can find a wealth of information about companies. Today, many companies are posting their profiles on social media sites, such has LinkedIn and Facebook. You can get a better picture of the company's employees, facilities, on and off campus activities, working environment and culture by viewing the posts and pictures on these sites.

There are also websites that provide reviews of companies by their current or former employees, such as Glassdoor (glassdoor.com), RateMyEmployer (ratemyemployer.ca), Kununu (kununu.com), JobAdviser (jobadviser.com.au) and TheJobCrowd (thejobcrowd.co.uk).

Before one of my scheduled job interviews, I used a search engine to find information about the company and discovered the company was losing money and was recently acquired by another company. This company location I was planning to interview at, which was once the headquarters, was now being run by another company that was downsizing their departments and personnel and moving their headquarters to another state. These were important events about the company that my staffing agency recruiter did not inform me about. However, I learned about these events before my job interview because I had done my research on the company. This information gave me better insight into the company; and helped me make a more informed decision on whether I should continue pursuing a job with this company or moving on to other more promising job opportunities. I chose to move on to another more stable company.

- **Company leadership:** Review the top brass—company President, Chief Executive Officer (CEO), Chief Financial Officer (CFO) and department leaders, especially leadership in your department (if you know the name of the department you could be working in). Once you are hired, you will no doubt hear these names again or possibly get a visit from them while you're at work. This information is usually found in the *"About Us"* or *"Who We Are"* sections of the company website.

- **Company address:** You can verify the company address the recruiter gave you with the address on the company website. If the company's home page does not provide the company address, look in the *"Contact Us"* section of the company website.

If the recruiter gave you the company name but not the address, looking up the company's name with an online search engine is a good way to find the address.

Rest assured, once you have secured an in-person job interview with the company, the staffing agency recruiter or company HR rep will ensure you have the company's address.

Having the company's address, particularly knowing what city the company is located in, will help you decide if the company's location is within your desired commute. I've refused many job opportunities from recruiters simply because I did not want to drive so far through congested traffic to the city where the job site was located.

If you are willing to commute to where the company worksite is located, and you are asked to come in for an in-person job interview, the company's address will also help you determine how long it will take you to drive, take a bus, train or subway to your job interview from your home to ensure you arrive on time.

The Hiring Manager and other Interviewers

There are always two things that hiring managers and other interviewers are looking for during your job interview:

- Your cultural fit
- Your technical or professional fit

Your Cultural Fit

Your cultural fit determines your ability to fit in and work well with the members of your new team once you are hired. Culturally fit involves your appearance, personality, enthusiasm, interests, sincerity and attitude that's on display while you are interviewing for the job. Your cultural fit also involves your social skills, oftentimes referred to as soft skills. Hiring managers always consider how well they think candidates can fit in socially with their company and their team when considering each candidate for the job. This is your cultural fit.

Rarely do hiring managers select a candidate for the job based solely on their "technical" or "professional" fit in the company. Technical or professional fit is your experience, knowledge and understanding of the job that you show you possess during your job interview as you answer technical or profession questions related to the job description.

Oftentimes the staffing agency recruiter or account manager who arranges your job interview will provide the names of one, some or all of the people who will be your interviewers along with the location, date and time of your scheduled job interview. If the recruiter or account manager does not provide you any names of the people interviewing you, ask the recruiter or account manager to get you the names of your interviewers.

Just as you would research the company, you can research your interviewers on social media sites, such as Facebook or LinkedIn. By researching the interviewer's social media posts, you can find out what things the interviewers are interested in; their hobbies, favorite sports or sports teams; and their recreations or places they've visited or vacationed at. This information can aid you in developing a rapport more quickly with the interviewers; and gives you the opportunity to show them what areas or interests you may have in common with them.

By bringing up things your interviewers are interested in or connected with when the opportunity presents itself, you cause the interviewers to see you more as someone they can connect with and get along with at work instead of "just another candidate" with no connection to them. This small connection will help influence and convince your interviewers that you would make a good cultural fit on their team than other job-seeking candidates because of the things you have in common.

Information posted by your interviewers on social media sites, such as LinkedIn, may also provide you valuable information about the interviewer's education, certifications, professional/technical background and previous jobs or companies they've worked at. All of this information about your interviewers allows you to connect with your hiring manager or other interviewers while they are considering your "cultural fit" during your job interview.

When is the best time to mention things you have in common with the interviewers? You can bring these things up at the beginning of your job interview during the introductions when you are asked by the hiring manager to tell the interviewers about yourself.

After the hiring manager introduces everyone and tells you about their company, he or she will then ask you to tell them about yourself. This does not mean the hiring manager is asking you to go through a long-winded timeline of your past job history. This is not what the hiring manager or the interviewers are looking for when they ask you to tell them about yourself. When the hiring manager says to you, "*Tell us a little bit about yourself*", the manager is not simply asking you to tell them about your professional/technical background only (your professional/technical fit). The hiring manager is also asking you to tell them a little something about your personal background too—your cultural fit—during your introduction.

The way you should tell the interviewers about yourself is through the lens of your professional/technical fit in fulfilling the requirements outlined in the "job description" and your cultural fit to give an indication on how you might interact with your potentially new team members. Researching your interviewers helps you identify things to say about your cultural fit that the interviewers can identify with. We'll cover each of these areas—professional/technical fit and cultural fit—in greater detail later in this and the next chapter.

Research the Job Description

Another piece of information I mentioned you need to get from the staffing agency recruiter is the job description showing the responsibilities the person in that available position will perform.

Oftentimes, a recruiter will email you a small portion of the job description—perhaps 3 or 4 lines—when they first contact you. If the description is too short for you to make an informed decision about seeking an interview for that job opening, you should ask the recruiter to send you the full job description. I've asked recruiters many times to email me a longer job description which they have done for me.

Comparing What You Know with the Job Description

First of all, the job description will reveal if you are capable of working in that job. The job description will tell you whether you even want to work in a job with the requirements listed in the description. The job description should give you enough information to make your decision on whether or not to move forward with the recruiter in submitting your resume to the hiring manager.

Don't be intimidated by everything you see in the job description. Hiring managers don't expect you to know everything listed in the job description. Rarely is a person capable of knowing or doing everything listed in most job descriptions, especially in highly technical positions.

The question you should ask yourself is: *Can I do most things in the job description and would I enjoy learning the rest of the things I don't know?*

If your answer is yes, you should go for it and allow the job recruiter to submit your resume to the hiring manager to get a job interview. Very few people know everything listed in job descriptions. In today's fast-paced growth of technology, you are not going to know every concept, process, application, device, machine, equipment, material or configuration out there. Nobody is that smart, and nobody has the time, energy or money to learn everything. Hiring managers know this too. What hiring managers want is someone who would be a good fit—*technically/professionally* and *culturally*—on their team; someone who knows or can do the majority—*not all*—of the items on the job description; and is willing to learn the things they don't know.

Use the Job Description to Determine Your Review

The second reason for asking for the job description is it reveals the subjects the hiring manager or other interviewers will be asking you questions about. The job description is like a summary or overview of the type of questions that will be on a test in school.

If the job recruiter submitted your resume for an interview with the hiring manager for a job opening, review the job description carefully and identify areas that are your strong points; areas that you are weak in; and areas you don't know. Focus your review on areas you are familiar with first. Brush up on those subjects, reviewing and familiarizing yourself with those subjects. Once you've completed that review, research and learn as much as you can about areas in the job description that you have little or no familiarity with. This may simply require you to read books or do some research online.

Basing your areas of review, study or research on areas that are your strong points, areas that you are weak in and areas you don't know will help you be more prepared to answer technical/professional questions that the interviewers will ask you. This will also translate into you feeling more confident and less fearful of the job interview.

Your Resume for the Job Interview

Ensure the Hiring Manager has Your Latest Resume

Before you give the hiring manager a copy of your resume, you should always check your resume one last time for editing. This is your one last chance to make sure the hiring manager and other interviewers see only what you want them to see on your resume.

In your job interview, you will not only be tested on your knowledge and experience about the items in the "job description"; you may also be asked questions about items that are in "your resume". Actually, anything you put in your resume is free game for interviewers to ask you questions about if they want to. Your resume may have been sitting at online job boards for quite some time; and it may have been a while since you last looked at your resume. It might contain things you do not want the hiring manager or other interviewers asking you questions about.

This should be an important reminder to you that you should only put items in your resume that you can confirm and talk about in a job interview. There's nothing worse than having the hiring manger or another interviewer point out a specific item in your resume and then start asking you questions about it when the only answer you can give them is the deer in the headlights look. Therefore, make sure you edit and trim your resume accordingly for the job you are interviewing for. Give your resume one last review and edit it accordingly before handing it over to the hiring manager.

Resume Reviews Prepare You to Discuss Past Work History

Sometimes, interviewers will ask you questions about certain sections of your resume. A good review of your resume before your job interview will help you recall and talk more confidently and comfortably about the Work History section of your resume if the hiring manager or other interviewers ask you questions about your past work.

When hiring managers ask you about previous jobs you worked at, use that as an opportunity to toot your own horn about yourself. The goal here is to show the hiring manager why he or she should hire you instead of someone else. I'm talking about making yourself stand out among the other candidates the hiring manager plans to interview for that same job. You do this by showing how what you've done in the past translates well into what is required in the "job description".

Your next source of income is on the line in this job interview, so this is not the time to be bashful, humble or shy—talk about yourself. Your hiring manager expects you to toot your own horn to make yourself look good in his or her eyes during your job interview. It's all part of the job interview process.

The proper way to toot your own horn about yourself is by briefly telling the hiring manager and other interviewers how your contributions at any former jobs you've held resulted in positive impacts for the company, workplace or customers. By reviewing your resume for things you did at previous jobs, you will be able to more quickly and easily remember and point out those things you accomplished at previous jobs.

When one of the interviewers asks you about past work, answer in a way that shows the hiring manager how what you did at that previous workplace saved time, energy or money; improved documentation, processes or ways to do things better; met critical deadlines or shortened delivery times; increased productivity or revenue; satisfied customers, managers or stakeholders; helped inform, educate or train personnel; or troubleshot or repaired things that restored or allowed continued service to customers or the mission. These are just a few of the things you can talk about when tooting your own horn about yourself in your job interview.

Certifications and Experience over Education in Job Interviews

Many people on the job market are finding out that having a degree doesn't necessarily guarantee you a job. In many career fields, it is certifications that trump a degree; and many times, experience trumps a degree and certifications. Other than checking off a box for some positions requiring a degree, it is certifications or experience that rule supreme over college degrees in many job interviews.

As someone who has worked in various jobs over 3 decades, it never ceases to amaze me how impressed and fascinated staffing agency recruiters and hiring managers are with the certifications or experience shown on my resume instead of the degrees on my resume. Not once over the years of job-hunting have I ever had a job recruiter or hiring manager say to me, *"That's a really nice degree you have there"* or *"Your degree is really something to behold."* However, I can't count how many times both staffing agency recruiters and hiring managers mentioned how impressed they were about my certifications or experience in my line of work.

Here's the difference between a degree, a certification and experience to hiring managers:

- **A degree** just tells a hiring manager you *have the mental capacity* for the job.

- **A certification** tells a hiring manager you *possess the knowledge* for the job.

- **Experience** tells a hiring manager *you can do the job*.

It's amazing how much we invest in our education with so little return on that investment. You spend all that time, energy, money, sweat and tears over years of sitting on hard school chairs; handwriting or typing instructor notes until your fingers were numb; burning the midnight oil reading books, researching online and writing papers; buying expensive textbooks on a thin budget; taking classes on subjects you would never have taken if they weren't required; overcoming fear and trepidation while cutting your teeth on giving oral presentations; and dissecting every partition of your gray matter for answers to tests, midterms and finals.

Once that sheepskin is hanging prominently on your wall and given its proper place on your resume, what response do you get from recruiters and hiring managers for all that hard work? Wait for it . . . crickets. Nada, nothing, not a peep.

What you will hear often from job recruiters or hiring managers is, "*I noticed you have your* [fill in the blank] *certification*" or "*Your certifications are pretty impressive*" or "*I see you have experience in* [fill in the blank]". It is usually your certifications or experience that typically catches the eyes of job recruiters and hiring managers; and prompts them to interview you for the job opening. That's because, when it comes to many jobs, your certifications or experience say more about your "technical/professional fit" for most of these jobs than a college degree. This revelation should be welcomed information for those of you who think the person with the best or highest degree is the one who is going to get the job. That's just not true in today's world.

How many certifications should you have? I say as many as your budget, time and interests will allow. The more certifications you have on your resume, the more you will stand out among your competition in the eyes of hiring managers before you even step into that job interview room.

If you completed only a portion of multiple exams required for a particular certification, include the exams you passed in your resume even though you don't have the certification yet. This shows the hiring manager you are taking the initiative to improve your knowledge and skills; something interviewers, bosses and employers desire in their employees.

If this information is discouraging to you right now because you have little or no certifications, don't despair. Fortunately, your job interview is not based solely on your certifications. It is a combination of your experience and skillsets you've highlighted in your resume; your ability to answer technical/professional questions; and your cultural fit in the company that determines who gets hired. That combination helps to level the playing field for that available job opening. My job is to show you how to maximize all of those areas that don't require a degree, certification or experience within the dynamics of the job interview process to give you an edge over your competition and convince the hiring manager to hire you for the job.

Here's more good news for you: getting certified is not a one-time deal for one job interview; it should be a continuous goal throughout your entire career. The longer you are in your career, the more certifications you should be racking up along with your experience and skills. Take the time to get certified.

Listen to the Experts

Angela Duckworth earned her Ph.D. at the University of Pennsylvania where she is now the associate professor of psychology. She has been an advisor to the White House, the World Bank, Fortune 500 companies and to NFL and NBA professional sports teams. In 2013, Dr. Duckworth gave a TED talk on TED.com, a nonprofit organization that shares ideas about technology, entertainment and design (TED) worldwide. Her talk was titled *Grit: The power of passion and perseverance*; and it is also the title of her 2016 New York Times Best Seller book.

Dr. Duckworth and her team conducted extensive research across all levels of academia to find out the single factor that produces success. Her study revealed that *"one characteristic emerged as a significant predictor of success; and it wasn't social intelligence, it wasn't good looks, physical health, and it wasn't IQ. It was **grit**."*

Dr. Duckworth defines grit as *"passion and perseverance for very long-term goals"*.

Because of this passion, drive and determination that Dr. Duckworth calls grit, it is also possible to have great success in life, including in job interviews, without higher education. This is not a knock against higher education. Education has its place in society. By all means, pursue higher education if you have the time, money, opportunity and interest. But don't discount the power of pursuing your focused passion and interests in job interviews through experience and certifications instead of higher college education. Many people have become quite successful in life by pursuing their passion without higher education.

Need more proof? Of course you do because you're a thinking person. You're not buying the idea that higher education is not needed for success. You feel people like Steve Jobs or Mark Zuckerberg are gifted prodigies who were destined for greatness from birth; an aberration of the normal path to success; and that the rest of us mortals in society must develop our greatness and success in life through higher education.

Then how do you explain these other "mere mortals" who gained great success and wealth in life with only a bachelor's degree? If you think it's ludicrous to suggest you can become very successful in your career and obtain higher salaries without higher education, try convincing these following people:

- Donald Trump (Bachelor's in Economics)
- Barbara Walters (Bachelor's in English)
- Oprah Winfrey (Bachelor's in Speech and Drama)
- Conan O'Brien (Bachelor's in American History and Literature)
- David Letterman (Bachelor's in Broadcasting)
- George Lucas (Bachelors of Fine Arts)
- J.K. Rowling (Bachelor's in French and Classical Studies)
- Jay Leno (Bachelor's in Speech Therapy)
- Jerry Springer (Bachelor's in Political Science)
- Katie Couric (Bachelor's in English)
- Martha Stewart (Bachelor's in History and Architectural History)
- Stephen King (Bachelor's in English)

Passion plus value equals success

Create value to others and you create success. The entire job interview process is all about convincing the hiring manager you add "value" to his or her company and team. That value doesn't just come in the form of education. That value comes in the form of experience. That value comes in the form of certifications. That value comes in the form of the way you dress in the job interview. That value comes in the form of the way you present yourself in the job interview. That value comes in the way you answer questions. And value comes in the form of your passion, drive and determination you display in your job interview. Albert Einstein said, *"Strive not to be a success, but rather to be of value."* To hiring managers and other interviewers, your value to their company is a combination of your technical/professional fit and your cultural fit in their company that determines if you are hired—not just the value of a degree.

SUCCESS DOESN'T PLAY FAVORITES

Success is not prejudice or biased. Success doesn't care if you're well educated or have no education at all. Success won't pass up on you in favor of someone else because of your education, race, religion, gender or sexual orientation. Success doesn't consider whether you came from the ghetto or a golden palace. Success plays on an even playing field where all players—you and I—have the same opportunity to win.

This should bring great comfort and inspiration to you if you feel you are at a disadvantage because of your lack of education or your particular background. You're not at a disadvantage; you're in that group of successful people in life who became successful without college degrees or a life handed to them on a silver platter. There's really no excuse for you if you have little or no education to not chase after your dreams like everyone else. Don't let other people talk you out of your dreams; and especially, do not talk yourself out of your dreams. Go after your passion—success will follow.

Arrival at Your Job Interview

When the hiring manager invites you to come in for an in-person job interview, you will be provided the address to the hiring manager's building where your job interview will take place. If the staffing agency that is helping you is in your local area, the staffing agency recruiter or account manager might meet you for the first time at the interview site too; and may introduce you to the hiring manager or one of the interviewers who will bring you to the interview room.

One of the things you should do in your pre-interview preparation is make sure you know how to get to the job interview location from your home; whether it is by car, train, subway or bus. Once you have the company address, you should take a test drive (or test ride by train or bus if that is your mode of transportation) to the job interview site to see how long it will take you to get there; and if there are any roadblocks, construction or other unknowns or possible delays along the way.

Here's where you can make your first of many good impressions by ensuring you arrive several minutes early before your interview time. The key here is you want to give yourself enough time to comfortably make it to your job interview on schedule with a few minutes to spare. You should arrive at the company building at least **10–15 minutes** early. However, you should not announce your arrival to your interviewers until **5–10 minutes** before your job interview start time.

I can't tell you how many times I drove a practice run from my home to the job interview site, only to discover obstacles that would have made me late to my job interview, such as traffic congestion on a busy street; the road was blocked or under construction; the road I planned to take ended up in a hotel parking lot (sounds funny now but I would not have been laughing if this happened to me on the day of my interview); or the company name had changed on the building of my job interview.

Do yourself a favor and discover these surprise obstacles and delays before the day of your job interview. It will ensure a stress-free commute to your job interview and will start your interview day on the right foot.

Introductions in Your Job Interview

The whole purpose of your job interview is to show your hiring manager and other interviewers that you are a much better choice than the other job-hunting candidates they are interviewing for the same job. You do that by showing you are a better ***technical/professional fit*** and ***cultural fit*** than the other candidates. One of the best ways to show your technical/professional fit and cultural fit for the job is right at the start of your job interview in your introduction of yourself to your interviewers.

Our focus in this job interview preparation section on introductions will concentrate on what you will prepare to say about yourself to your panel of interviewers after the hiring manager or team lead asks you to *"Tell us a little bit about yourself."* These are some of the most terrifying words to people who fear job interviews. Rest assured, I'm going to show you exactly what you need to say to calm your nerves and help you shine before your interviewers. This is one of my favorite parts of the job interview—introducing myself—because I've learned what things to say ahead of time. You're going to know what to say ahead of time too.

Tell Us a Little Bit about Yourself

Most job interviews consist of either the hiring manager only or 2–6 people accompanying the hiring manager. Usually, the more technical/professional the position they're looking to fill, the more interviewers there are with the hiring manager in the job interview.

There's usually one person leading the job interview, such as the hiring manager or lead person on the team you will be on if you are hired. The remaining interviewers in the room are usually members of the team you will be a part of when you are hired.

The hiring manager will start things off by introducing the other interviewers in the room to you; and oftentimes will break the ice by telling you a little bit about their company. Afterward, the hiring manager will ask you to tell them a little bit about yourself.

This introduction phase of your job interview is much too important for you to talk about yourself off-the-cuff or off the top of your head. You must have a well-prepared introduction that you've gone over with a fine-tooth comb to ensure every word you speak carries weight during your introduction.

You want to use your introduction as an opportunity to stand out from the other job-seeking candidates by incorporating certain things from your past jobs (your technical/professional fit) and your personal life (your cultural fit). By using your introduction to show how your past job experiences relate to the "job description" for this open position, and by sharing a few things about your off-work activities or personal life, you will already be scoring huge bonus points toward successfully completing your job interview before answering a single question.

How to Prepare Your Introduction for Your Job Interview

You should write out what you are going to say about yourself with an emphasis on your technical/professional fit and your cultural fit for this job opening. It's best to do this on a computer so you can quickly and easily save, update, edit and tailor your introduction for each new job interview in the future.

Once your introduction is well-thought-out and written down, you should begin memorizing and verbally practicing what you are going to say about yourself until you can give your introduction (without reading it) in a relaxed, normal and smooth pace. Later in this section, we'll cover roll-playing which is a good way to practice being in a job interview giving your introduction to your hiring manager and other interviewers.

Technical/Professional Fit and Cultural Fit in the Introduction

In the previous section on researching your interviewers, I mentioned that when one of the interviewers asks you to tell them about yourself, this is not a request for you to give them a long-winded account of your past work history from beginning to end. The hiring manager and other interviewers are looking for something specific when you are asked to tell them about yourself.

The two things interviewers are looking for in your introduction:

1. Your **technical/professional fit** in their company and team.

2. Your **cultural fit** in their company and team.

The hiring manager is asking you to tell them things about your skill sets that can translate to accomplishing the "job description" of the person they want to hire; and to tell them things about you as a person that would make you a good cultural fit on their team and in their company. Therefore, the way you should tell the interviewers about yourself is through the lens filter of your technical/professional fit to fulfill the job description and your cultural fit to fit in with your new team members and the company culture.

Instead of starting out with some boring, long-winded story such as, *"It all started when I was born in the hills of West Virginia . . ."* or *"My first job was working as a paper boy in the busy metropolis of New York City . . ."*; take what you've learned from your review of the job description and start telling the interviewers specific things you've learned or done in past jobs that relate directly to those items in the job description. This will convince the hiring manager that you are a good technical/professional fit for the job before they even ask you technical/professional questions. Then continue on and tell them something personal about your life—your hobbies, trips, passions or interests. Try to include something you noticed your interviewers are interested in after researching their social media profiles or just share something in general to make an emotional or social connection with your interviewers. This will help convince your interviewers that you will be a good cultural fit on their team.

How long should you talk about your technical/professional fit and cultural fit during your introduction?

You should spend about **1–2 minutes** talking about your **technical/professional fit**; and about **15–30 seconds** to talk about your **cultural fit** during your introduction. If you get nervous when talking about yourself in job interviews, you should breathe a big sigh of relief because that's only a couple of minutes of tooting your own horn. This is not a lot of time; so make every word count. You don't want to talk long in your introduction. A long-winded introduction only tells the hiring manager and other interviewers that you talk too much; and they will probably pass over you for another candidate for the job that they believe won't talk their ears off at work.

Include Technical/Professional Fit in Your Introduction

When talking about your technical/professional fit for **1–2 minutes**, share how things you've done in past jobs relate to the responsibilities in the job description for this new job opening they are trying to fill. For example, if the job description mentions certain pieces of equipment, tools or processes, share how you worked with those same or similar types of equipment, tools or processes in past jobs. If the job description requires knowledge and experience in certain office skills or office software, talk about past job experiences where you used those same or similar types of office skills or software. If the job description asks for a person who can operate certain machinery, heavy equipment or vehicles, share how you operated those same or similar types of equipment in previous jobs. If the job description states the need for a person who can design, engineer, implement or test certain things, talk about how you performed these types of duties in former positions. If the job description requires you to provide leadership, training, mentoring of junior personnel or to interact with customers, talk about how you handled these same or similar types of responsibilities for previous companies.

When you talk about these things you've done in past jobs, make sure you include how what you did had an ***impactful result*** for that team, workplace or company. As you talk about past work experience, tell the interviewers how what you did at previous jobs saved time, energy or money; improved processes, documentation or drawings; met critical deadlines or shortened delivery times; increased productivity or revenue; satisfied customers or stakeholders; supervised, mentored, educated or trained personnel; and troubleshot or repaired critical components that restored or allowed continued service to customers or the company mission.

Don't waste your hiring manager's time talking about past job experiences that do not relate directly or indirectly to the "job description" when you're emphasizing your technical/professional fit for **1–2 minutes** during your introduction. There is also no need to mention things such as your certifications or degrees because these are plainly shown in your resume. However, you can talk about any on-the-job training you received in the past that is related to the "job description". You need to use those precious couple of minutes to show what "*value*" you bring to their team or company. You do this by talking about specific technical/professional knowledge and experience you have that fulfills the job description—your technical/professional fit; and by displaying social skills that make them feel you would be someone they would like to work with on a daily basis—your cultural fit. That's what makes you someone of value to them; and it will help you stand out above all the other job candidates interviewing for the same job as you.

Include Cultural Fit in Your Introduction

Your cultural fit is where you take about **15–30 seconds** to include something about your personal life; something that is not related to the "job description". This is where your research into the interviewer's or the company's social media posts, such as on Facebook or LinkedIn, can be helpful. When talking about your personal life, try to include something you read about in the interviewer's and company's social network profile. You don't have to mention that you read their posts or saw their pictures engaged in those same interests. Just mention that that's one of your interests if it is.

However, it's not absolutely necessary that you know something about your interviewers in order to share something personal about yourself. Simply take a few seconds to share something personal about you to show them you not just a "candidate"; you are a person with a life. This will help make that social connection with them—your cultural fit.

Take **15–30 seconds** during your introduction to talk about something in your personal life that might interest your interviewers that shows a social side of your life—your cultural fit on their team and in their company. You can share your interests, hobbies, sports, places you like to visit or vacation; books you enjoy reading; music you enjoy listening to; or volunteer work you enjoy doing.

If the hiring manager or another interviewer asks you a question such as *"What are you passionate about?"* or *"How do you spend your free time?"* or *"What do you do for fun?"*, they're actually trying to get to know you personally and find out if you have anything in common with them "socially"—your cultural fit. I've been asked all of these questions in job interviews. So don't be surprised or put off by these types of questions. They just want to know you more as a person instead of as just another job-seeking candidate.

What's so important about sharing your personal life or interests—your cultural fit?

When you are hired, your work area, desk or cubicle at your job site is most likely going to be right next to the people who are interviewing you. Many hiring managers or other interviewers just want to know if you'll fit in well with them on a daily basis since you'll most likely be around each other all day long. Use your introduction as an opportunity to mention things that will give your interviewers some assurance they will enjoy working alongside you. So, if you found some information about the interviewers on social media, use that information to mention personal things about yourself that they might be interested in, such as a favorite sport or sports team they identify with; hobby, talent or pastime they're interested in; a book they enjoyed reading; a movie they enjoyed watching; or a place they vacationed or visited. If you couldn't find anything about the interviewers on social media posts or if you were not given the interviewer's names; you should still mention something about your personal side in your introduction to show your cultural fit.

You may consider or discount this advice as over the top with too much emphasis on *"who"* you are rather than *"what"* you can do. With all due respect to your career accomplishments, keep in mind that you're probably not the only job-seeking candidate with that degree, that certification, that knowledge and experience or that skill set. There are several job-seeking candidates in front of you and behind you in that job interview line with similar qualifications and skill sets as you who can do the same things as you in that job. When all candidates look similar in what they can do in the eyes of the hiring manager and other interviewers, you can be sure they're going to lean heavily on each candidate's cultural fit to determine which candidate they would most likely enjoy working with all day long.

With so much information out there on social media, why not take advantage of this profile information and make it work to your advantage over your competition in the job interview process? Remember, every word you speak in those couple of minutes of your introduction counts for or against you in your job interview—use that brief opportunity wisely.

Job Interview Questions and Answers

Interview questions for all jobs fall into one of two areas:

1. Your **technical/professional fit** for the job.

2. Your **cultural fit** for the company and your team.

The topics you see in the job description that you get from a staffing agency recruiter, company website or HR department are the areas where the hiring manager and other interviewers will be asking you technical/professional questions. How well you answer those technical/professional fit questions will determine if they hire you *for the job*.

The topics you normally don't see in the job description that hiring managers and other interviewers oftentimes ask job-seeking candidates questions about are areas concerning your cultural fit for the job. Cultural fit questions cover your soft skills; your ability to communicate and interact with other people; your behavior or response when working in teams or groups; your ability to take criticism, feedback or advice; how you handle difficult bosses, co-workers, customers or other pressures on the job; or how well you can problem-solve issues and provide solutions.

How well you answer these cultural fit questions will determine if they hire you *for the team* you'll be on and the company you'll work at.

Notice that **technical/professional fit** questions relate to hiring you for *the job*. **Cultural fit** questions relate to hiring you for *the team*.

Technical/Professional Fit Questions in the Job Interview

Obviously, the technical/professional fit questions that the hiring manager and other interviewers ask job-seeking candidates will be different for each person's career and each type of job in that industry. Therefore, I won't be able to provide the answers to those questions that each person reading this book will encounter.

However, I would suggest that after you've gone through a job interview; always take the time afterward to write down as many questions you can possibly remember that the interviewers asked you. You'll discover over time, after interviewing with several companies in the same line of work, that many hiring managers and other interviewers in different companies ask the same questions. By writing down these job interview questions related to your particular career field, you'll have the best reference source to review technical/professional questions when preparing for your next job interview.

Having been through numerous job interviews over the years, I've begun to notice the similarities in the questions being asked by different interviewers at different US government agencies and private corporations where I interviewed for jobs. I started taking notes on these questions, such as what questions were asked; which questions I knew; and which ones I didn't know. I did this until it got to the point where I had several pages of these notes from job interviews.

Whenever I had to prepare for a job interview, I would always go to these notes first; and afterward I would review books or online material as needed to complete my review based on the job description for a particular job opening.

When I identified items on the job description that were new to me, I would study those areas and began anticipating questions that interviewers would ask me; and then I created questions and answers for those subjects too.

As a result of all these notes from interviews and self-study, I had hundreds of pages of questions and answers to choose from for job interviews that I reviewed based on the job description. I put these technical/professional questions and answers for job interviews in several volumes of books I wrote titled *IT Questions & Answers For IT Job Interviews*.

Cultural Fit Questions in the Job Interview

A working environment is a team environment. Therefore, hiring managers are looking for people who will contribute to the company's goal of establishing and maintaining a healthy team environment; not hurt, ruin or undermine team cohesiveness and a positive working environment. Hiring managers try to bring in people to their company that will contribute to a healthy working environment by asking cultural fit questions during the job interview process.

Over the years, I also collected a series of cultural fit questions that hiring managers and other interviewers have asked me in many job interviews and that I have asked people when interviewing them for both US government and corporate jobs. In this section, I cover all of these cultural fit questions and show you how you should respond to these questions.

These cultural fit or soft skills questions and answers cover a wide range of questions that hiring managers and other interviewers may ask to give them a better understanding of how you might behave, interact with and respond to different people and situations in the workplace. Questions such as *"Who was your most difficult supervisor and why?"* or *"Explain a workplace experience with a difficult person and how did you deal with them"* are intended to help hiring managers uncover your behavioral tendencies in your interpersonal relationships with co-workers under stressful or difficult situations at work. Your answers to these questions help hiring managers determine your cultural fit, also referred to as your social qualities, soft skills or emotional quotient (EQ) in the workplace. In the next chapter, I'll explain in greater detail what your emotional quotient is and how it comes into play during your job interview.

Some people refer to these social qualities as *how you are wired*, but that makes it sound as if these qualities are permanently hardwired in you and cannot be changed; when in fact, these are social skills that you can develop and improve.

During your preparation for your next job interview, take the time to go over these cultural fit questions and prepare well-thought-out answers in advance that show the hiring manager you can handle difficult social situations in the workplace with confidence, maturity and professionalism.

Cultural Fit Questions and Answers

Here are some actual cultural fit or soft skills questions that hiring managers or other interviewers may ask you in your job interview. After each question, I provide insight into what hiring managers are looking for when asking each question; and some suggested answers to these questions. This way, you can answer each question the way you want to after you understand what the hiring manager is looking for when asking the question. Keep in mind that all of these questions that interviewers ask are used primarily to help them determine your cultural fit in their company; not your technical/professional fit.

How You Should Respond to the Weakness Question

One cultural fit question that is sometimes asked in job interviews is **"What is your greatest weakness?"** Sometimes this weakness question is asked in different ways, such as the following:

- **Question:** What is your greatest weakness?
- **Same Question:** What area do you need to improve on the most?
- **Same Question:** Name one thing about yourself that needs improving.
- **Same Question:** What is one thing your previous boss, supervisor or manager would say you need to improve on?
- **Same Question:** Tell me about a time when you failed.

This weakness question is a bit tricky to answer because you are trying to put your best foot forward in the job interview. The last thing you want to do is talk about something that places you in a negative light in front of the hiring manager or other interviewers; and makes you look worse than other job-seeking candidate interviewing for this job. We all want to show our better selves, not our darkest angels.

What is a bad response to the weakness question?

The last thing you want to do is ignore preparing for this question, hoping you will never encounter it in a job interview; only to find yourself fumbling for an answer when you are asked to share your weakness. You should also not try to sidestep this question by telling the hiring manager you can't think of any weaknesses or you don't have any weaknesses.

The hiring manager is asking this question knowing full well that everyone has weaknesses and that each person is aware of most of them. To deny you have weaknesses or to suggest you can't think of any weaknesses makes you appear as if you are disingenuous; you have something to hide; you didn't prepare well enough for the job interview; or you are too proud or conceited to accept or acknowledge the fact that you have weaknesses just like everyone else. Avoiding this question makes you appear insincere or too sensitive; as someone who may not accept feedback or constructive criticism well in the workplace.

Any attempt by you to sidestep this question reveals a weakness in you in the eyes of the hiring manager—something you were trying to avoid all along. Instead, why not answer this question properly on your own terms in a way that makes you look good—something you are trying to do throughout your job interview.

Most people who attempt to answer this question about their weaknesses try to put a positive spin on it by using false weaknesses such as, *"I'm too organized"* or *"I'm a perfectionist"* or *"I'm a workaholic"*. This is an old worn-out trick that hiring managers see right through as a poor attempt to make yourself look good by inserting words, such as "organized" or "perfectionist" or "workaholic", into the picture of your weakness. Nice try, but that is a failure in answering this question properly.

So, should you just spill your guts about every nook and cranny of your dark side and worst habits to the shock and horror of everyone in the room? Of course you shouldn't. There's no need to turn your answer into a freak show, horror film or a *Saturday Night Live* skit. You also don't want to mention weaknesses in areas where it is necessary or crucial for you to function properly in that job.

Hiring managers who ask this weakness question are gauging your self-awareness, your honesty and sincerity about your limitations and your ability to overcome your weaknesses and limitations through self-improvement. After all, there will be times in the workplace that everyone feels weak or inadequate for a new challenge. That's all part of the growth process in the workplace.

The answer you want to provide your hiring manager is a carefully crafted answer that reveals one of your weaknesses or flaws that is not a deal-breaker in your job interview. Something that can be fixed or developed; and that you are in the process of fixing and developing in your life. Don't mention a weakness that you are doing absolutely nothing to fix, develop or improve, such as watching too much sports on TV. (No wait, I think that's a strength, not a weakness.)

A deal-breaker weakness is something about you that would hurt your chances of being hired for that particular job. Some examples of deal-breakers are stating you don't like working with people; you can't control your temper and tell people off at work; you have a tendency to ridicule people; you get bored, tired or sleepy on the job; you steal supplies from work or people's lunch from the refrigerator (this one should be a crime punishable by law); you're not a morning person and you have a hard time getting up in the morning which makes you late for work at times; you don't like working overtime or unscheduled longer hours; you fart a lot at work (another crime that should be punishable by law); you are a poor speller or reader; you can't handle pressure; you tend to complain a lot at work; or you tend to freeze up and remain quiet in meetings, discussion groups or collaboration sessions.

So how do you respond to the weakness question?

Pick a weakness that is still acceptable and tolerable in the workplace that you are working on to develop and improve. Here are some examples of weaknesses you can use while showing your self-improvement efforts to fix or improve on:

- You need more leadership skills but you are reading more about developing leadership qualities or taking leadership classes.

- You lack skill or experience in a particular area but you are studying or practicing that area more.

- You get nervous in job interviews but you try to overcome these nerves by preparing more or practicing interviews through role-playing and positive visualization techniques as much as possible.

- You've been late to meetings because you lose track of time at work because you pour yourself into your work. Therefore, you try to always calendar your meetings and set reminders as soon as you are scheduled for one (every hiring manager can identify with this weakness).

- You can be too frank or direct at times but you are aware of it. Therefore, you're studying more on proper communications skills, personality types and how to properly influence or interact with people.

- Sometimes you'll spend more time than necessary on a project because you can be too critical of your own work, leaving yourself with less time to complete the project before the suspense date. However, you're trying to learn not to waste so much time checking and rechecking things too many times and by studying time management skills.

Other Cultural Fit Questions and Answers

- **Question:** Who was your most difficult supervisor and why?
- **Same Question:** Tell me about a time you had to work with a difficult person on your team.
- **Same Question:** Explain a workplace experience with a difficult customer and how did you deal with them.
- **Same Question:** Have you worked with someone you didn't like? If so, how did you handle that situation?

- **Explanation/Answer:** These questions really aren't about the difficult supervisor, co-worker or customer. The hiring manager is not inviting you to start bad mouthing former co-workers; play the blame game; or start throwing people under the bus, backing the bus up, and then running them over again for good measure. Step away from the gas pedal.

  These conflict questions are about *you* and how *you* handle conflict, difficult people or difficult social situations in the workplace.

  With these types of questions, the hiring manager is checking your interpersonal skills, referred to as soft skills or people skills. The hiring manager is trying to gauge your habits, attitudes, tendencies, oral communications, teamwork, problem-solving skills and emotional quotient (EQ) when dealing with difficult people and social situations to determine if you are a good employee and amicable person worth selecting to work on their team.

It's important that you formulate your answer in a way that shows you can maintain a mature, professional and positive behavior in difficult social situations resulting in **positive results and outcomes**. If you had some bad bosses or co-workers in past jobs, don't ever call them bad bosses or bad co-workers. Instead say they were challenging or difficult bosses or co-workers.

The wrong way to answer this question is responding to conflict *with* conflict. You do not want to appear as the type of person who would escalate the conflict further in the workplace or someone who turns into a raging Hulk at the slightest provocation.

Instead, you want to show how you can *de-escalate* conflict in the workplace. Show how you are willing to communicate professionally during conflict; and how you're able to come to healthy positive resolutions of conflicts. Show the hiring manager how you will take the high road in resolving conflicts.

Most people have had or will have some form of conflict at work. If you've experienced conflict at a previous job, you can use one of your past experiences with conflict as an example to show how you handled it maturely and professionally.

Go over these three areas when talking about a workplace conflict in a previous job:

1. Pick a specific example of conflict you experienced at a past job. The conflict does not have to involve you directly. It could be two other people in conflict at work.
2. Talk about how **you** responded to the conflict in a mature, professional manner. Share how your words or actions de-escalated the conflict.

3. Then share how your mature, professional response to the conflict helped (not hurt) the situation.

If you haven't experienced conflicts in past workplaces, you can tell the hiring manager that you've been fortunate to have had great bosses and co-workers to work with in your past jobs; that you and your co-workers had mutual respect for one another; and that you got along well with everyone in your former jobs.

If you can answer the conflict question in one of these ways, you will pass this question properly with flying colors.

- **Question:** Who was your best supervisor and why?

- **Explanation/Answer:** This question really isn't about your best boss, supervisor or manager. It is about *you* and how *you* interact with people, particularly with workplace management and authority.

With this question, the hiring manager is checking your interpersonal skills, primarily your perspective on "supervision" and "authority" that will make you a good employee and compatible to work with. It's important that you formulate your answer in a way that shows you can maintain mature, professional and positive behavior interacting with both management personnel and your peers within a workplace setting.

Use this opportunity to show the hiring manager you know how to give compliments and praise to other people in the workplace—bosses or co-workers. Feel free to talk about bosses or co-workers you enjoyed working for or working with; and give specifics about what you liked about the person. Show the hiring manager that you are the type of person who speaks well of people and likes to give people pats on the back. Hiring managers like this because it shows you can bring a positive attitude and positive vibes to the workplace. People who are upbeat and positive are the type of people employers like to bring into their company culture.

- **Question:** Do you prefer to work independently or on a team?

- **Explanation/Answer:** There is no right or wrong answer to this question because it is good to be able to work either independently or on a team.

  Stating you enjoy working independently shows you are confident in your abilities; however, if you only like working independently, this makes the hiring manager think you are not a good team player.

  Stating you enjoy working in a team shows you are a team player; however, if you only like working in a team environment, this makes the hiring manager think you are not confident in your own abilities to accomplish tasks on your own.

  Therefore, the safe way to answer this question is to tell the hiring manager you like both. Tell the hiring manager you enjoy working in a team environment, but you also enjoy working independently when the job requires you to do so. By telling the hiring manager you are comfortable working both on a team and independently, you make yourself appear as a person with a broader, more dynamic and complex mix of qualities for the job. This means you add *value* to the job.

- **Question:** Explain a workplace situation where you had to think outside the box.

- **Explanation/Answer:** This question really isn't about the inside or outside of the box. It is about *you* and how well *you* process, manage and solve difficult or complex situations or problems. With this question, the hiring manager is checking your abilities in problem-solving, acting as a team player, flexibility, adaptability, creativity, innovativeness, initiative and working well under pressure.

  This is another opportunity for you to stand out above other job-seeking candidates because you get to talk about a challenging issue at a past job where you used your problem-solving skills, creativity, innovativeness or adaptability to solve the problem. It doesn't necessarily have to be an experience where you had to think outside the box; just an experience where you had to *think*. It could be a problem that required careful thought process, insight, investigation, research and application by you to make things work at the time in that previous job. Again, show how what you did provided **good results with a positive impact** for that situation.

- **Question:** Where do you see yourself in 5 years?
- **Same Question:** What are your long-term career goals?
- **Same Question:** Where do you see yourself in the future?

- **Explanation/Answer:** This question might come across as odd in an age where many professionals are ready to move on to their next job in 3 to 5 years. The important thing to recognize in this interview question is that hiring managers want to know if you are interested in staying long term with their company and workplace.

It costs their company time and money to hire you (such as going through the job interview process and paying a hefty commission to a staffing agency), and it will cost their company time and money when you leave because they have to pay with time and money to find your replacement. Therefore, some hiring managers want to know if you will give their company some return on their investment after hiring you; or do your career goals indicate that you will potentially leave their company in the near future—1 to 3 years from now.

Hiring managers also know that job-seeking candidates that seek long-term relationships with their company are more likely to be more productive workers. Any job-seeking candidates who reveal they plan to move on from their company in a couple of years are oftentimes the first to be eliminated from the job interview selection process.

Therefore, even if you don't plan on being with that company long-term, tell the hiring manager you hope to be **with their company** long-term or 5 years from now (if the hiring manager asks you where you plan to be in 5 years). Remember, there may be 5–15 other applicants waiting in line to interview for that same job as you. When faced with equally qualified job-seeking candidates, hiring managers are more inclined to select the candidate that will provide the greatest return on their company's investment.

It's unrealistic in our 21st century to expect any job-hunting candidate to still be with a company beyond 5 years. So, you're just answering the hiring manager's unrealistic question and expectation with an equally unrealistic answer. However, the fact is you, the hiring manager or anyone else doesn't know if you'll be with that company after 1, 2 or 5 years; unless, of course, you know how to work a crystal ball. Who knows, you may like it there and decide to stay beyond 5 years or work there until you retire.

So rather than laughing in the face of the hiring manager for asking you this outdated question, simply pat yourself on the back for the hiring manager's interest in wanting you to stay at that company long-term. Just play along with the hiring manager's silly reindeer game; take a deep breath of gratitude; and then give the hiring manager the assurance he or she needs with a positive answer that indicates you plan to give their company a return on their investment. You can share other long-term goals you may have; just make sure they include *their company* in your long-term plans when asked this question.

Remember that this is a question directly related to your tenure with this company, not something about your personal life you are sharing during your introduction. Therefore, the goals you share should show how they will make you a better worker for their company. In other words, do not share personal goals that have nothing to do with the job opening or the company when this question is asked of you. Your goals are in competition with the goals of other candidates seeking that position who are asked this same question. The job interview is all about showing you have more *value* than those other candidates seeking that job. Don't waste this opportunity sharing goals that don't make you appear as a better choice than the other candidates.

If you have a problem with this approach to answering this question, just remember this one thing: You could easily be more qualified than the other candidates they will interview for this job opening; however, this company won't hesitate to pass over you because you suggested you will not commit to the company's ball and chain beyond 1–3 years.

Here are a couple of ways you can answer the goals question:

- *I hope to gain further experience in this company that will allow me to excel in this position, and becoming one of your top performers and continue to advance in this company.*

- *My long-term goals are to stay with this company, continue growing in knowledge and experience that will not only benefit me, but also benefit your company and your customers.*

- **Question:** What are you passionate about?
- **Same Question:** What do you do for fun?
- **Same Question:** How do you spend your free time?

- **Explanation/Answer:** When you are hired, your work area, desk or cubicle will most likely be right next to the people who are interviewing you for that job. Because of this, the hiring manager and other interviewers just want to know if you'll fit in well with them on a daily basis.

The hiring manager and other interviewers also like knowing you are not just another worker who can do the job. They want a well-rounded person with a life outside of work. Someone who might even possibly have interests outside the workplace that are similar to their lives outside the workplace. That means they're trying to see if they will connect better with you in the workplace than the other candidates seeking this job.

Here are some suggestions to make a cultural fit connection with the hiring manager or other interviewers when answering this question:

- Share your interests, hobbies, sports, places you like to visit or vacation; books you enjoy reading; music you enjoy listening to; a talent you enjoy developing, such as painting, singing or writing; or volunteer or charitable work you enjoy doing.

- Try to include things you read about in the interviewer's and company's social media profile. This is where your research into each interviewer's or the company's social media posts, such as on Facebook or LinkedIn, will be valuable as I previously mentioned.

- **Question:** Why do you want to work here?
- **Same Question:** Why are you here?
- **Same Question:** Why are you interested in this job?
- **Same Question:** Why should we hire you?
- **Same Question:** Why do you think you will be successful at this job?

- **Explanation/Answer:** Hiring managers use this question to not only ask you about your interest in the open position; they are asking you about your interest in their company; and they want to know what you have to offer the company.

Your answer to this question should include two things:

1.   What attracted you to this **job** for *this* **company**.

2.   What you have to offer this company.

Share what attracted you to this job for this company: Use the job description and what information you learned about this job online to explain what attracted you to this type of job. Share your interest and enthusiasm in the company mission, people, working environment, equipment, processes, tasks or other aspects about the job description that made you want to work there. Use this opportunity to share how you enjoyed or performed these same aspects of the job description at previous jobs.

The research you performed on the company will provide you several good reasons for why you want to work for the company. This is a good opportunity to show you've done your research into the company by sharing what you learned about the company culture, mission, industry, accomplishments or awards that attracted you to it. Let the hiring manager know that you like his or her company; and that you're impressed with the company's accomplishments, awards and press releases.

Share what you have to offer this company: Use the job description and what information you learned about the company to explain how your knowledge, experience, skill sets or training fit in well with this job; how you will be able to contribute to the company to produce positive results and impacts; and how you believe or know you will be successful in this job.

- **Question:** Why did you leave your last job?
- **Same Question:** Why do you want to leave your current job?
- **Same Question:** What were your reasons for leaving your last job?

- **Same Question:** Why didn't you remain' at your last position?
- **Same Question:** What was it about your last position that made you decide to move on?

- **Explanation/Answer:** Hiring managers know candidates seeking work are like a box of chocolates: *You never know what you're gonna get.* That's why you can expect hiring managers to ask this prying question into your reasons for leaving your current or last job. They want to know if you're as good as Milk Duds or just a dud. Are you as refreshing as sweet cold lemonade on a hot summer day or are you just another angry, sour lemon bringing your problems to their company? Are they getting another good employee or someone's worst nightmare?

    Your goal when answering this question is to ensure the hiring manager that you're the real deal when it comes to being a quality employee worth hiring. You want to show the hiring manager that you are a stable, reliable and responsible employee.

    Regardless if you didn't like your current or previous job, boss, co-workers, customers or salary; don't provide your hiring manager negative reasons for leaving your job. If you tell the hiring manager you are leaving or left your job because of the people or money; your hiring manager will automatically assume you won't like the people or salary in this new job either. In other words, the hiring manager will scratch your name off the list of people they would hire.

    Give the hiring manager positive reasons for leaving your job. Show the hiring manager that you are leaving or left your job for the **right** reasons—not for the **wrong** reasons. Make your answer more about moving on toward something *positive* rather than about leaving something *negative*. Remember, hiring managers are comparing you with other job-seeking candidates to determine which person they're going to hire. Don't give them a reason to eliminate you from the competition for the *wrong* reason.

You should start your answer off by telling the hiring manager some positive things you like about your current or last job, and then proceed to tell them positive reasons for why you plan to leave or left that job.

Some examples of positive reasons for leaving a job include looking for a more challenging job; you are looking for a position that will allow you to develop and broaden your skills or provide you more growth potential in your career; you weren't able to utilize all of your talents in your current or previous job, so you felt it was time to move on to opportunities that allow you to contribute more to a company with your skill sets; you've outgrown your current or last position and are looking for new ways to continue growing in your career; although you enjoy your job, you need to find a job closer to your home with a shorter commute time; you were working on a 6-month or 1-year contract; and when the contract ended, you decided to take some time off to hone your skills, work on some other personal projects or hobbies, complete some certifications, take some vacation time off or do some traveling before heading back into the workforce.

By the way, whenever there are large gaps of time in-between jobs, you should always try to answer this question by showing you were working on *self-improvement* during your time away from work, such as reading, studying or researching areas of your career field, taking classes, developing your skills through practice, working on certifications, attending workshops, self-employment activities, volunteer work, and so forth.

You can also include the answers from the previous question "about "*why you want to work at their company*", such as sharing what attracted you to this particular job or their company, and what you have to offer their company. Make the hiring manager feel as if his or her company and this available position is your dream job; a much better opportunity than your previous job.

Questions to Ask the Interviewers and Closing the Job Interview

When your job interview is about to conclude, the hiring manager or another person leading your job interview may ask you, "***Do you have any questions for us?***" Don't take this question lightly and pass on this opportunity out of fear of asking any questions. The hiring manager and other interviewers actually expect you to ask them some questions. If you do not ask them any questions, you show a lack of preparation for this job interview or lack of interest in their company. If you don't ask any questions, it will cause you to miss out on another opportunity to stand out one last time above the other candidates who are interviewing for this same job.

The entire job interview process is about you making yourself stand out above all the other job-seeking candidates that the hiring manager will interview; and this closing part of your job interview is as equally important in your focus on accomplishing that goal. Use this opportunity to show the hiring manager you're interested in this job and that you have given this job serious enough thought to have come up with your own questions about this job opportunity.

Ask the Right Questions in Your Job Interview

Prepare **2–3 questions** ahead of time that you can ask the hiring manager based on your research of the company or areas where you can contribute to their team. Ask smart, thoughtful questions that are focused on how you can contribute to the company, fulfill the job description or enhance their team. Always try to ask the hiring manager open-ended questions rather than questions that can be answered with a simple yes or no.

I usually type my questions on my computer; print them out, and take them with me to my job interviews. When hiring manager asks me if I have any questions for them, I'll simply take out this list of questions and start asking my prepared questions.

The following list is suggestions on the types of questions you can ask the hiring manager or other interviewers in your job interview (pick only 2–3 questions to ask):

- *Can you share some of the hot issues, projects or immediate needs you have going on that you expect the person filling this job to help with?*

  When the hiring manager tells you about projects or needs that his or her team or company has; think about any knowledge, experience or training you have in any of those areas; and continue the conversation by telling them how what you did at past job/s can help meet those needs.

- *Based on my resume and my responses in this interview, can my skill sets help with your team right away?*

  As the hiring manager tries to answer this question, this prompts the hiring manager to quickly consider how your skill sets can be used to fill the current needs on their team. It also lets the hiring manager know you are eager to get started with contributing on their team.

- *For the person you select for this job, what are the most important things you want that person to accomplish their first 60 days on the job?*

  Again, this lets the hiring manager know you are serious and eager to get started with contributing on their team.

- *I've researched your company website and noticed a lot of positive things about your company, such as* [name some positive things you read on their company website]. *What do you like most about working for your company?*

This not only shows you did your homework by reviewing their company website and were impressed with what you read; you also complimented them by telling them positive things you read about their company. Now they get to tell you what they like most about their company. This is a win-win question for you, the hiring manager and other interviewers in the room.

Just as there are questions you should ask in a job interview, there are also questions you should not ask. Asking the wrong questions in a job interview shows you didn't do any research on the company or are more focused on what the job can do for **you** than what you can do for **them**.

When it comes to asking questions in a job interview, take some sage advice from President John F. Kennedy's Inaugural Address in Washington D.C. when he became the 35th President of the United States. President Kennedy said, *"Ask not what your employer can do for you; ask what you can do for your employer."* (Ok, President Kennedy used the word "country" instead of "employer", but you get the idea.)

Bringing up the wrong topics in the form of these following questions in job interviews tells hiring managers you did not come prepared for the interview or are more interested in yourself than in fulfilling the requirements of the job. Asking poor, shallow or selfish questions will easily turn off the hiring manager and lessen your chances of being selected above other candidates for the job.

Here is a list of questions you should NOT ask hiring managers during your job interview:

- **Questions that are answered by reading the job description.** This implies you did not take the time to thoughtfully read the job description. Asking these types of questions make you look like you didn't care enough about the responsibilities of the job to read the description in detail. Get the job description from the staffing agency recruiter before your job interview; then review it completely.

- **Questions related to what the company does that are answered by simply reading the company's website.** This implies you did not care enough about their company to do your homework and research their company website.

- **Questions related to money (your compensation).** Asking questions about salary or compensation implies you are more interested in the money than in the job.

- **Questions related to company benefits.** Examples are questions about health or dental insurance, vacation, training and education, perks and discounts. Asking questions about company benefits implies you are more interested in the company benefits than about the job.

- **Questions related to promotions, transfers to other teams or the possibility of working a second part-time job.** These types of questions imply you aren't going to stay with their team for very long. It shows you are not 100 percent focused on this job opportunity.

- **Questions about working remotely by telecommuting from home instead of coming in to work.** These types of questions imply you don't like working with customers, colleagues or leadership; or lack the available schedule or discipline to work within your scheduled working hours.

- **Questions related to drug testing, background or reference checks, the company's policy on marijuana, Internet use or monitoring of social media profiles.** These types of questions imply there is something wrong or inappropriate in your life or behavior that you do not want the company to know about.

- **Questions related to working hours, working late or on weekends.** These types of questions imply your schedule might not fit into the working hours required for this job or you are less inclined to make sacrifices to make it to work for odd hours when the work situation requires you to be there. You don't want to come off as a person who is always watching the clock at work, ready at the top or bottom of the hour to leave work for the day. Ask the job recruiter these types of questions if you found this job through a staffing agency. Otherwise, once you are hired, you will be told your working hours; and may be given the opportunity to flex your hours or work remotely from home on occasion.

- **Questions about why the previous person in this position left this company.** This question implies you're being nosy. Regardless who previously filled this position and the reasons for their departure; this information is none of your business in the company's eyes.

- **Questions relating to negative things about their company.** These types of questions imply you do not hold their company in high regard. Just as you are trying to put your best foot forward in the job interview, so is the hiring manager. Don't bite the hand that feeds you or step on the feet that greet you.

Your Closing Statement at the End of Your Job Interview

Immediately after the hiring manager has answered your **2–3 questions** at the end of your job interview, take the initiative to add some closing statements to make one last good impression on the hiring manager and the other interviewers in the room. Don't wait for the hiring manager to ask you for closing statements because he or she won't. Just add them in the conversation immediately after the hiring manager has answered your questions at the end of your job interview.

There are two things you need to prepare to say in your final closing statements:

1. Thank the hiring manager and other interviewers.

2. Ask for the job.

The first thing you want to do at the end of your job interview is thank the hiring manager and other interviewers for taking the time out of their busy schedules to interview you for this job. Let them know you appreciate them giving you the opportunity to be interviewed by them. Gratitude goes a long way when it comes to your *cultural fit* in the eyes of the hiring manager and other interviewers.

The second thing you want to do in your closing statement is ask for the job. The greatest salesperson in the world will not make a single sale until they ask for the sale. If you don't ask, you can't have. After everything the hiring manager has told you about the company; after all the interview questions they asked you; let the hiring manager and other interviewers know you are still interested in this open position, and that you are still enthusiastic about working with them.

You could combine both the thank you and asking for the job in a couple of closing sentences. You could say something simple such as the following:

I'd like to take this time to say thank you to all of you for taking time out of your busy day to interview me. I'm very interested in this job, and I would enjoy working with all of you on your team.

By simply letting the hiring manager and other interviewers know you're interested in the job and would enjoy working with them is telling them you want the job—this is a big deal. That's all they needed to hear from you to reassure them you still want the job and are excited about working with them after being grilled by them with so many questions. They can't tell you on the spot that you've got the job because they most likely have to interview other candidates after you.

Don't say, "*I want this job*", because those words make you appear desperate and it sounds like you just want the job and don't care about working with them.

Don't ask, "*When can I start?*", because that makes you come across as arrogant and as if you blindly presume you've already beat out all the competition before all the competition has had a chance to interview for this job.

Role-Playing Job Interviews

Role-playing is an important part to job interview preparation. Role-play is especially beneficial if you are new to the job interview process; haven't done an interview in a while; or always seem to be nervous or apprehensive in job interviews.

Role-play exercises allow you to act out an imaginary situation that mirrors a real situation to make you feel more natural and comfortable with that situation when it is happening in real life. The more times you go through role-playing job interview exercises, the more natural and comfortable you will be when it comes time to go to an actual job interview.

Practice Role-Playing with People You Know

By role-playing job interviews with someone you know, you give yourself the opportunity to practice your job interviewing skills in a friendly, safe, non-threatening, relaxed, controlled environment. Role-playing the job interview allows you to gauge and assess how you actually perform in a job interview without being in an actual job interview. It helps you identify your strengths and weaknesses while acting out the job interview. Role-playing gives you the opportunity to receive critiques from trusted family members or friends that are helping you in the job interview role-play; and allows you to make the necessary changes and improvements to your job interviewing skills after each role-play. All of these benefits of role-playing the job interview can anywhere at any time before the real job interview takes place.

To perform job interview role-playing, you take the role of the job-seeking candidate and one or several other people you feel comfortable with will play the role of the hiring manager or other interviewers. Use your family members, roommates or friends to help you with this role-playing exercise. You can even use your children or younger siblings and relatives as the hiring manager or other interviewers.

As the job-hunting candidate, start with your prepared introduction; then have the person or people playing the role of hiring manager or other interviewers ask you questions. At the end of your job interview role-playing, have the person in the hiring manager role ask you if you have any questions for them when they are done asking you questions. That's when you should ask the hiring manager your prepared questions. Once they've answered your questions, immediately end the job interview by thanking the hiring manager and other interviewers for their time and let them know you want the job.

Have fun with these imaginary job interviews and learn to relax, smile and enjoy role-playing the job interview. The more you relax and enjoy these role-playing exercises, the more relaxed and comfortable you will be in actual job interviews. Role-playing allows you to shake off those nerves or rust (if you haven't interviewed for a job in a long time) in the privacy of your own controlled environment with family or friends before going into a real job interview.

Don't forget that smiling and laughing is allowed in job interviews. I've smiled and laughed with hiring managers and other interviewers in a lot of actual job interviews. Smiling and laughter in a job interview is usually a good sign that you and your interviewers are connecting with each other—an important aspect of *cultural fit* for getting hired for the job. Just don't laugh for any reason in your actual job interview—that means you're crazy. However, if someone said something funny during your job interview, show your lighter side by laughing appropriately if someone cracks a joke in your job interview. Laughing shows your hiring manager and other interviewers you'll be fun to work with; not someone who is too serious all the time. Don't go overboard with your laugh, such as making snorting sounds or loud vociferous noises when laughing. As with your attire and appearance, keep your laughter in moderation.

In job interview role-playing, you should select a comfortable place where you can pretend being in the job interview room, such as in your dining room, living room, dorm room or any other place where there is at least two chairs and table. No need to make things complicated while role-playing. If you want, you can simply have a couple of chairs facing each other.

Read through this entire chapter and the following chapter before performing role-playing exercises for job interviews.

The following list is some of the things you should include in your job interview role-playing:

- Your initial greeting and handshake with the hiring manager or other interviewers you first meet at your job interview. (This is covered in more detail in the next chapter.)

- Your entrance into the job interview room and taking your seat. Most job interviews are in a small meeting room with a table and chairs. The job-seeking candidate usually sits on one end of the table and the interviewers sit side by side on the opposite side of the table. If you don't have a table in the room you are practicing in, that's fine. Just use chairs and sit opposite of each other.

- Your posture and attitude when standing or sitting. (This is covered in more detail in the next chapter.)

- Listening to the hiring manager introduce the other interviewers and sharing about his or her company. Since this about *you* and not the interviewers, give the person role-playing as the hiring manager a ready-made sheet they can use to introduce the other imaginary interviewers and talk about their imaginary company. (This actual process is covered in more detail in the next chapter.)

- When the person in the hiring manager role asks you to share some things about yourself, go through your "prepared" introduction that includes your *technical/professional fit* and your *cultural fit*. Take **1–2 minutes** talking about your **technical/professional fit** and **15–30 seconds** to talk about your **cultural fit**.

- **Answering questions from the hiring manager or other interviewer/s.** Use a checklist of questions that the role-playing hiring manager or other interviewer can ask you. You can make several lists of questions if you have more than one person role-playing as the interviewer. If possible, try to list items that are in the job description or general items in your career field that the hiring manager or other interviewers might ask. (This is covered in more detail in the next chapter.)

- When the hiring manager asks you if you have any questions for them at the end of your job interview role-playing, ask your "prepared" questions.

- After the hiring manager answers your questions, immediately thank the hiring manager and other interviewers for their time and let the hiring manager know you are interested in the job (ask for the job) and would enjoy working with them. (This is covered in the in more detail in the next chapter.)

- Repeat this job interview role-playing as many times as you can until you feel comfortable and confident with your job interview performance.

- Most importantly, have fun doing this. You and your family or friends helping you should enjoy these role-play exercises. The more you enjoy these exercises in practice, the more you'll enjoy these job interviews in real life.

Invest in Your Children's Future—Role Play

After you've practiced this role-playing as the job-seeking candidate several times, you can do something really special. If you're role-playing with young family members, such as children or young adults, reverse the roles and let your younger family members be the job-seeking candidate. By allowing younger family members to experience being interviewed in the job-seeking candidate role, you will be providing them with one of the most important life skills they will be using throughout their adult life. Why not get them use to the idea of interviewing for a job in a fun, safe family atmosphere. There's an old proverb that says, "*Start children off on the way they should go, and even when they are old they will not turn from it.*" Proverbs 22:6 NIV

Even the US Military Performs Job Interview Role-Playing for Their Departing Military Members

Role-playing the job interview is so important to successfully passing job interviews that even the US military uses these role-playing techniques when helping service members transition back to civilian careers. Each branch of the US military has a transition assistance program (TAP), a program mandated by Congress and implemented by the Department of Defense in partnership with the Labor Department and Veterans Affairs. TAP training helps military members that are preparing to leave the military to successfully transition back to civilian life and start a new career.

Part of the TAP program are employment workshops provided by the Department of Labor that teaches departing military members valuable lessons on how to be competitive in the job market; covering topics such as employment, training and education opportunities, resume writing, job search strategies, goal setting, interview preparation, negotiating their salary and other job-hunting skills. This training gives our military members the best chance for success in seeking civilian jobs.

When I was in the US Air Force serving my last tour of duty at Ramstein Air Base in Germany, the time had come for me to prepare to retire from the military and return to civilian life. To help prepare me for my transition, I went through the Air Force TAP program.

One of the most beneficial TAP workshops I enjoyed taking part in was the job interview role-playing workshop. This workshop split all of us military participants in groups of two. One person would play the part of the interviewer and the other person was the job-seeking candidate.

After we received lessons from our job counselors on best practices for job interviews, we each took turns interviewing the other person as if we were the hiring manager; and then we would reverse roles and would take a turn at being the job candidate who was being interviewed. Each time we completed our interviews, we and our instructors would provide feedback to each other about our performance as the job candidate.

At first, all of us felt a bit nervous and apprehensive as we went through the role of the job candidate being interviewed. As we repeated this role-playing, we each got more comfortable and confident with talking to our imaginary hiring manager; showcasing our skill sets; incorporating our past work history in the conversation; answering interviewer questions; and highlighting how we could be a positive contribution to a company.

Thanks to those job interview role-playing sessions in that TAP workshop, I felt very comfortable and confident in job interviews after leaving the military; and I've enjoyed interviewing for jobs ever since.

PART TWO

DURING THE JOB INTERVIEW

CHAPTER SIX

It's Game Day—The Job Interview

All our dreams can come true—if we have the courage to pursue them.
Walt Disney

During the Job Interview

Everyone Gets a Little Nervous Before Game Day

It's perfectly normal to feel a little nervous before or during your job interview. Everyone feels a bit nervous before an important event in their life. Lawrence Peter Berra, better known as "Yogi" Berra, a Major League Baseball player, manager and coach for the New York Yankees was an 18-time All-Star and 10-time World Series champion while a player. When it came to being nervous, he said, *"I always got nervous the nights we played in the World Series. First pitch, I was nervous. Then after that, forget it; I'd start playing."*

Sure, it takes a little courage to walk into that job interview room. But what is courage anyway? It is simply doing things even when you're afraid. Mark Twain said, *"Courage is not the lack of fear. It is acting in spite of it."*

Major League Baseball player Babe Ruth is famously known for hitting 714 home runs in his career. In 1923, he broke the record for the most home runs in a season and broke the record for the highest batting average. Do you know what other record Babe Ruth broke that year? He struck out more times than any other Major League Baseball player that year. Babe Ruth struck out 1,330 times in his career; a Major League record for strikeouts that he held for 30 years; and was known as the king of strikeouts during his career. So what did Babe Ruth have to say about striking out? He said, *"Never let the fear of striking out get in your way."*

Sure, you may strike out a few times during job interviews—so what. Everyone strikes out now and then, even Babe Ruth. Don't let the fear of striking out get in the way of you going at bat again in another job interview and hitting a home run next time. John Wayne said, *"Courage is being scared to death—and saddling up anyway."*

In this chapter, I'm going to show you how to saddle up, *pilgrim.* We all have to do things in life that sometimes make us nervous or afraid. The good news is that the more we prepare, practice and do those things; the easier and less fearful those things become. So, think of your next job interview as simply a favorite sport or game you like to play; and as you know, the more you play a sport or game, the better you are at it.

I want you to think of me as your greatest fan in the stands cheering you on; and think of me also as your couch on the field with you helping you win in the game of life; particularly in job interviewers. I believe in you. I know you can do this. You're going to succeed at this job interview because you're a champion. You've got what it takes to shine and succeed in your job interview.

I realize that for most of you reading this book, the thought of you having to go through a job interview is an intimidating, oftentimes fearful experience—statistics have proven this to be true for most people. To some people, the job interview seems like such an unbearable or impossible feat. Instead of trying to eat that whole elephant of fear in one bite, let me show you how to eat that elephant one bite at a time. Conquering your fears usually require taking small necessary steps that eventually take you to the top of that impossible mountain you thought you could not reach. Francis of Assisi said, *"Start by doing what is necessary, then what is possible, and suddenly you are doing the impossible."*

I'm going to show you the necessary steps to help you forget your nerves one step at a time as you start focusing on the top of that mountain—successfully passing your job interview. I'm going to show you how to get rid of your fears of job interviews by beating those nerves into submission so you can feel as confident and comfortable as possible during your job interview. I'm also going to show you what things you need to say and do during your job interview so you stand out among all the other job-hunting candidates who are interviewing for that same job so the hiring manger selects you over your competition. We'll start with an overview of the job interview process.

An Overview of the Job Interview Process

Most job interviews last an average of one hour from the time your scheduled interview starts to the end of your job interview when the hiring manager is walking you back to the front entrance of the company building. For starting positions at fast food restaurants or some retail stores, your job interview may last only 30 minutes. If your job interview goes past one hour, it is usually a good sign that the hiring manager is interested in you. A much shorter than normal job interview for a particular job is usually an indication that things are not going so well. When the hiring manager purposely cuts the job interview short, it is because the hiring manager is not pleased with the performance of the person being interviewed.

Any time there is more than one job interview step in the employer's job interview process, it is a good sign each time you are invited back for the next succeeding job interview. If this is your case and you are invited back, take a moment to pat yourself on the back for a successful performance each time you are invited back by the hiring manager for the next level of the job interview process. When you are invited back, this is not a time to worry; it's a time to feel good about how you did in the previous job interview.

Your ultimate goal during your job interview is to show and convince the hiring manager and other interviewers in the room that you are the best fit—*technically/professionally* and *culturally*—for their company and team members, many of whom may be interviewing you in that room.

By "**technical/professional fit**", I mean you have to answer the technical/professional questions well enough to convince the hiring manager you have the "hard skills" to do this job well. Your technical/professional fit determines how well you fit with the responsibilities outlined in the "job description".

By "**cultural fit**", I mean your appearance, behavior, personality, enthusiasm, interest, sincerity and attitude you display in your job interview to convince the hiring manager you have the right "soft skills" (social skills) to fit in and work well with the members of your potential new team when you are hired for the job.

Hard skills define your level of technical/professional ability to perform the job. Soft skills define your level of social skills to fit in and interact with your co-workers, managers and customers.

Measuring your cultural fit does not mean that the moment you enter the job interview room, someone is going to hand you a personality test to complete. What this does mean is that while the hiring manager and other interviewers are asking you technical/professional questions to determine your hard skills related to the job description, they are silently observing your soft skills; your cultural fit as they watch how you appear in their eyes; and how you respond to any soft skills questions.

This means that your technical/professional fit (hard skills) is observed **objectively and unbiased** by the hiring manager and other interviewers—you either know the answers to the technical/professional questions or you don't. The hiring manager's personal feelings, emotions and opinions do not come into play in your answers to any technical/professional questions.

Your cultural fit (soft skills), on the other hand, is observed **subjectively and biased** by the hiring manager and other interviewers—their opinion of you is based on their own individual perspective of what makes a person a good fit on their team or in their workplace. The hiring manager's sense or judgement of your cultural fit is based on his or her personal feelings, emotions and opinions.

The good news about the job interview process is that you may not be the best technically/professionally fit candidate for the job (other candidates may answer the technical/professional questions better than you), but if you showed a much better cultural fit for the job (you made the hiring manager and other interviewers feel they would get along better with you than with the other candidates being interviewed), the hiring manager may be more likely to pick you than the other candidates.

The bad news about the job interview process is you may be the best technically/professional fit candidate for the job (you may have answered all the technical/professional questions better than all the other candidates), but because you weren't the most culturally fit person for the job (you made the hiring manager and other interviewers feel they would not get along better with you than with another candidate being interviewed), the hiring manager is more likely to pass on you and pick another candidate for the job opening.

Your qualifications and skill sets—your technical/professional fit—are what got the attention of the staffing agency recruiter and the hiring manager; and ultimately got you the job interview. But your social skills, your soft skills, your cultural fit is what may be the deciding factor in getting you hired for the job.

Hiring managers need to be pleased with what you know about the job (technical/professional fit), but they also need to like who you are as a person (cultural fit) in order to select you for the job above all the other candidates interviewing for that job. Your task during the job interview process is to make the hiring manager and the other interviewers like you both as a technical/professional person who can do the job as well as a person they would enjoy working with. My job is to help you accomplish both with the information I will provide you in this chapter.

The list below is the key areas you should focus on *during* your job interview:

- Arrival at your job interview

- Introductions in your job interview

- Intelligence quotient (IQ) versus emotional quotient (EQ) for job interviews

- The importance of attitude in your job interview

- Power posture, power thoughts, power words and power prayer for job interviews

- Other factors that impact your job interview

- Job interview questions and answers

- Questions to ask the interviewers and closure

Arrival at Your Job Interview

It's Game Time—Be on Time

Arrive early to your in-person job interview but not too early; no more than **5–10 minutes** early. If you let the hiring manager know you've arrived 15 minutes or earlier before the start time of your job interview, the hiring manager will most likely feel inconvenienced rather than impressed by your "too early" arrival. The hiring manager and other interviewers are most likely trying to wrap things up with what they're doing at work before your arrival; and now that you let them know you've arrived sooner than expected, they'll either feel uncomfortable about making you wait longer or will have to stop what they're doing and come out to greet you. Either way, it won't start your job interview on the right foot like you thought by arriving too early.

It's good to arrive at the company building **10–15 minutes** earlier to make sure you get there on time, but you can wait in your car until **5–10 minutes** before the start time of your job interview so that you don't announce your arrival too early to the hiring manager.

Turn your cell phone off, including the vibrate mode; or better yet, leave your phone in the car prior to entering the employer's building. One of the worst impressions you can make during a job interview is having your phone go off or the hiring manager seeing you look down in a response to the vibration going off or a text coming in. They'll all know what that look means—it means you don't care enough about your job interview to shut off your phone. In that case, your job interview is probably already over for you without you even realizing it.

Arriving at a US Government Agency on a Military Installation

Going to a job interview for a US government agency on a military installation presents a few challenges in both getting on the military installation as well as into the government building. Do not fret; there is a process in place to get you on the installation for your job interview.

You will not be allowed to enter (walk in or drive in) most US military installations without a military ID card (active or retired military), Common Access Card (CAC) or an escort.

CAC cards are issued to active duty uniformed service personnel, Selected Reserve, DoD civilian employees and eligible contractor personnel. Once you are hired as either a US government civilian employee or contractor, you will be issued a CAC card that is valid for the length of your employment or contract to allow you to enter the military installation without an escort.

Contractor CAC cards are distinguished by a green bar across the front of the card. This CAC card will also provide contractors limited use of other services on the military installation, such as shopping at the military shoppette store (a small convenience store) or filling your car with gas at the gas station.

If you do not have a military ID card or CAC card, someone from the government facility will have to meet you at the front entrance of the military installation to escort you in to your scheduled job interview.

Most military installations have a Visitor Center outside one of their gated entrances. The Visitor Center is where you can get a temporary visitor pass to enter the military installation, but you'll need an authorized person with the proper ID credentials to sign you in to get your pass. Therefore, the Visitor Center is where you will most likely meet the person who will escort you to the government agency building where your job interview will take place. These Visitor Centers usually have seating areas, restrooms and a drinking fountain while you wait for your escort to arrive.

Keep in mind that this whole escort process takes time that might make you late for the start of your job interview. Therefore, find out from either the staffing agency recruiter or from one of the interviewers (the recruiter will provide you a contact phone number for one of the interviewers at the government agency) what time should you meet your escort at the Visitor Center.

Introductions in Your Job Interview

Staffing Agency Recruiter Meets You at Your Job Interview

When you arrive at the hiring manager's building on the day of your job interview, you might be greeted by your staffing agency recruiter or account manager if their staffing agency is in the local area of the building where you will be interviewed. The recruiter or account manager will let you know if they plan to meet you at the job interview location. If your staffing agency recruiter or account manager is there to greet you when you arrive, that person will oftentimes remain with you until the hiring manager or someone else comes out to greet you. Sometimes both the staffing agency recruiter and the account manager will be there to meet you; sometimes only one of them will be there; but most times no one from the staffing agency will be at your scheduled job interview.

A meeting with staffing agency personnel at your job interview is oftentimes the first time you will meet the people who helped you get that job interview. Use that opportunity to personally thank them for their help in getting you that job interview.

Meeting the Reception Desk at Your Job Interview

If no one from the staffing agency will meet you at your scheduled job interview location, the person you will most likely meet first is the person at the reception desk of the building where your job interview is held. If you are interviewing for a job at a retail store or some other business where they don't have a reception desk, then you may be meeting the hiring manager first. If there is at a reception desk at your job interview location, let the person at the reception desk know you have an appointment with the person whose name you were given for the job interview.

If the person at the building's reception desk is the first person you meet, make a good first impression by smiling and being friendly with that person. There's no need to shake the receptionist's hand but always be courteous and friendly with the receptionist. You'd be surprised how many people the receptionists know and talk to in that building. If you treat the receptionist rudely or as if they don't matter, the receptionist can let your hiring manager or other interviewers know of your unprofessional behavior which will reflect poorly on you in their evaluation of your *cultural fit* for their company. Your cultural fit in a company also has to do with how you interact with and treat everyone in the company, including the receptionist.

The same holds true for the person who meets you at the Visitor Center of a military installation to escort you to your job interview. This person who escorts you onto the installation is oftentimes a member of the interview team or the team you will be on when you are hired.

Your Initial Greeting at Your Job Interview

When greeting someone, extend your hand, look them in the eye, smile and give them a firm handshake. Do not give one of those soft, sheepish or wet noodle handshakes. A limp, weak grip in your handshake makes you appear weak, disinterested, insecure or negative. A firm, strong handshake makes you appear strong, confident, assertive, interested and positive.

When greeting the hiring manager or other interviewers, smile and give them a pleasant greeting, such as *"Hi, I'm* [state your first name only]. *It's nice to meet you."*

Depending on the complexity of the job you are interviewing for, different types of personnel could possibly be in that interview room with you, such as a hiring manager, a team lead, and several team members. Typically, all of these individuals are members of the team you will be part of when you are hired. If everyone is standing while you are meeting each person, give them the type of handshake and greeting I previously mentioned (you only have to mention your name once to the first person).

If you are seated with everyone else, and someone else enters the interview room and takes their seat; there's no need to go over to them and greet them. You can simply say hello from your chair. If that person who enters the room comes over to you to greet you while you are sitting down, stand up first and greet them with a handshake as I previously mentioned before taking your seat again.

The Hiring Manager in Your Job Interview

The hiring manager is a manager in the company who requested the position for his or her team be filled—the position you are interviewing for. The hiring manager is also the person who makes the final decision on which job-seeking candidate will be hired for that job opening. The title of "hiring manager" is only temporary until the manager hires a person for that available job. Afterward, the hiring manager uses whatever title is their normal manager title instead of the "hiring manager" title. Depending on the size of the company, this manager could manage an entire section of teams in the company, a small portion of teams, or only one team.

The available position that the hiring manager is trying to fill is a position that is under the hiring manager's area of control and leadership. Therefore, although the manager puts in a "personnel request" to the company's HR department to fill the available position, the manager is the one who will take ownership of the hiring process, as the "hiring manager", for this position while the HR department supports and assists the manager along the way. The hiring manager will work with the HR department concerning creating the job description of the available position; conducting the resume reviews and job interviews; completing and finalizing the hiring, salary negotiations and job offer process for the selected person; and establishing the start date of the person they selected for the job. Since the person selected for the job will become a part of the hiring manager's team, this manager has a vested interest in ensuring the right person for the job is selected for his or her team members. That means a person who is the best technical/professional fit and cultural fit for the manager's team.

The hiring manager will most likely become the reporting manager for you and your team when you are hired for the job. The manager's office could be either in the same office you will be working in or located in another room or building.

The hiring manager could have strong background experience in your line of work; someone that possibly started at the level you're coming in at with this company and worked their way through the ranks until they reached the management position they are in now. The hiring manager could also be a person with little to no background experience in your line of work but possesses the necessary managerial skills to be in that position.

There are situations where there could be two managers in the job interview room with you; a manager for full-time company employees and a manager for contractors. If this is the case in your job interview, one of these managers will be your hiring manager depending on whether you are interviewing for the job as a company employee or a contractor.

Such was the case when I was interviewing for a job opening with a large company. This company normally hired job-hunting candidates as "contractors" first for a 6-month contract. If they liked the contractor's performance after 6 months, they gave the contractor the option to either continue working as a contractor or become a full-time company employee. Therefore, both the manager for the company employees and the manager for the contractors were present in my job interview.

If the hiring manager is present in your job interview, he or she will introduce you to all the interviewers in the room. The manager will oftentimes share a little bit about their company before asking you to tell them a little bit about yourself. Once all the introductions are out of the way, the hiring manager and the other interviewers will begin asking you technical/professional fit questions; and possibly some cultural fit questions. If the hiring manager does not have the same technical/professional background as you, he or she will pass the interview over to the other interviewers to ask you the technical/professional questions. Regardless if the hiring manager has your technical/professional background or not, you can be sure the manager will be observing you to determine if you are a good cultural fit for his or her team as you are being evaluated for your technical/professional fit.

The Team Lead in Your Job Interview

Each team of workers in companies usually has a team leader, referred to as the "team lead" or simply "lead". The team lead is the person who is the technical/professional leader on the team. This person is usually the senior experienced person on the team you will be on when you are hired; is the driving force behind the team; and is responsible to the manager for the rest of the team members, assignments, progress and accomplishments.

The lead person will delegate work assignments from the team manager to you and the rest of the members on your team; however, the team lead is responsible to the manager for the overall success of the team's projects and assignments. Since the team lead has experience in your particular technical/professional area, the lead may oftentimes work alongside you to complete an assignment, project or goal depending on the size of the project. If the team lead attends meetings on behalf of the team, the lead will pass on or brief you and the rest of the team on the minutes from the meetings.

As a matter of protocol, when you or other team members have issues to pass on or discuss with leadership, they first go through the team lead; then their team manager; and then to higher leadership.

When it is time to assess and evaluate your performance and the performance of other team members, the manager will seek inputs from the lead person about you and other members of your team. The lead may also fill in for the team manager's responsibilities when the manager is out of office.

Because of the team lead's responsibility for your team, it's normal to have both the hiring manager and the team lead in the room with you during your job interview. When the hiring manager cannot make it to your job interview, the team lead usually takes over and leads the job interview.

Giving Your Introduction in Your Job Interview

After the hiring manager introduces the interviewers to you, the last introduction during your job interview will be your "carefully prepared" introduction given to the interviewers. In the previous chapter, I covered how you should prepare and practice for giving this introduction. You shouldn't have to "think up something" from thin air. You should already know what you're going to say about yourself—this will help calm your nerves because you already know what you're going to say. Now it's time to put all that practice to good use in your actual job interview.

In your introduction, remember to talk about things in your past jobs that relate to the job description (your technical/professional fit); and mention one or two things in your personal life that the other interviewers might identify with and connect with (your cultural fit).

Remember, your entire introduction should only be **2–2 ½ minutes** long. That's not a long time; so relax—you can do this. Nobody knows you better than you, so smile and be confident introducing to these interviewers the person you've known all your life—*you*.

Introductions don't get any easier than that. You've prepared your introduction. You've practiced introducing yourself. Now just be your natural self as you talk about yourself. Nobody is asking you to be anybody else but yourself as you introduce yourself to your interviewers. Oscar Wilde said, *"Be yourself; everyone else is already taken."*

And remember, it's not always the smartest or most educated person who gets the job; it's the person who is the best fit—technically/professionally and culturally—that usually gets hired.

Intelligence Quotient (IQ) versus Emotional Quotient (EQ) for Job Interviews

For those of you who think the smartest or most educated job-seeking candidates are always going to trump all other candidates in a job interview and be the one who gets hired, think again. Since the 1990s, many scientists, psychologists, researchers and educators have been stating that your emotional intelligence (EI), also known as emotional quotient (EQ), and attitude are better predictors of your success in life, including in job interviews, than your intelligence quotient (IQ).

The Intelligence Quotient (IQ)

The intelligence quotient (IQ) is, at best, a rough measure of academic intelligence; the ability or capacity of a person to learn, understand and apply information and skills. The first IQ test was invented in 1908 by French psychologist Alfred Binet when the French Ministry of Education, who passed a law requiring all French children attend school, needed a way to determine which students were not benefiting from regular classroom education and needed remedial instruction.

Today, there are a variety of IQ tests available; and the test content in each of these tests differs widely from one another. One IQ test may show you only pictures of blocks, circles, triangles and other shapes; another IQ test may ask you questions about words and numbers; and still another IQ test may ask you questions about pictures, words and numbers. Regardless of the test used, the results of each IQ test, called

"IQ scoring measured in Intelligence Interval and Cognitive Designation" is pretty standard across the board regardless of which IQ test you take.

The results of your IQ test are normally compared to other people in your age group to determine your IQ score. You can take one of these IQ tests for free at many Internet websites.

Here are some online IQ tests you can take:

- https://iqtest.com/

- http://www.free-iqtest.net/

- http://www.myiqtested.com/

- http://www.seemypersonality.com/IQ-Test

- http://www.brainmetrix.com/free-iq-test

The Importance of Emotional Quotient (EQ) in Job Interviews

One might be led to believe the person who has the highest IQ is the one who will get the job or is the most successful in life. Unless you are being interviewed by Goggle or some other company that invests twice as much as other companies in recruiting people based primarily on the highest IQ or higher education (PhDs), many companies would rather consider a person's emotional quotient (EQ) and attitude over IQ and higher degrees in their hiring decisions. Today, many companies are incorporating EQ tests into their job interviews and adopting EQ training into their business culture.

Most people are familiar with IQ, but few people are aware of their emotional intelligence (EI), also referred to as emotional quotient (EQ). What's important to realize about EQ is that in many cases, employers will hire a candidate whose EQ is higher than their IQ.

Your EQ score rates your ability or capacity to perceive, understand, control, evaluate and express emotions—yours and other people's emotions. How you deal with your emotions determines how well you work with and get along with other people, particularly people in your workplace.

People with high EQ scores are considered confident individuals with good communications and leadership skills that have good control over their emotions. This makes them better suited for group or team environments, such as in the workplace, than people with low EQ scores—characteristics that the IQ scores does not measure or reveal.

Besides controlling their emotions well, people with high EQ scores are highly motivated and productive; face change, variety and challenges head on because they do not fear failure; and show greater endurance and perseverance under long-term struggles and hardship than people with low EQ scores.

If the definition of a high EQ score sounds strangely familiar to the definition of an alpha type person, you would be right because many of the qualities of a person with a high EQ score parallel the qualities of alpha types.

Just as there are IQ tests you can take online, there are many EQ tests and assessments on the Internet you can take for free.

Here are some online EQ tests you can take:

- https://memorado.com/emotional_quotient

- http://www.ihhp.com/free-eq-quiz

- https://www.arealme.com/eq/en

- https://www.mindtools.com/pages/article/ei-quiz.htm

- http://personality-testing.info/tests/EI.php

- http://greatergood.berkeley.edu/ei_quiz

- http://www.iq-test.net/eq-test.html

What the Experts Say about Emotional Quotient (EQ)

Travis Bradberry knows all about EQ testing and training. Dr. Bradberry holds a Dual Ph.D. in Clinical and Industrial-Organizational Psychology from the California School of Professional Psychology. He is a world-renowned expert in emotional intelligence, the award-winning coauthor of the 2009 book *Emotional Intelligence 2.0* and cofounder of TalentSmart, the world leader in emotional intelligence tests and training.

TalentSmart provides EQ resources to over 75 percent of Fortune 500 companies; and the talentsmart.com website provides many case studies showing how EQ training and tests have helped many companies.

TalentSmart's own studies of people at all levels of work in different industries of every region of the world reveal that 90 percent of your top performers at work have high EQ scores; and that people with high EQ scores also make an average of $29,000 per year more than people with low EQ scores.

When TalentSmart tested factors that predict a person's greatest chance for success in the workplace, they included emotional intelligence in addition to 33 other necessary workplace skill sets in those tests. The results revealed that of all these skill sets, emotional intelligence provided the strongest predictor of performance success—58 percent—in all types of job markets.

Dr. Bradberry points out that your EQ level is not fixed at birth; it can be developed, reshaped, improved and increased to produce positive impacts in your life. He states that the whole person is made up of IQ, EQ and personality; each independent of each other; and that of the three, only EQ can be developed and altered. Dr. Bradberry argues that you need to increase your EQ level to increases your chances of success in your career as well as all other areas of your life.

Daniel Goleman holds a Ph.D. from Harvard and is the author of the international bestsellers *Emotional Intelligence: Why It Can Matter More Than IQ, Working with Emotional Intelligence, Social Intelligence*, and the acclaimed business bestseller *Primal Leadership*.

In Dr. Goleman's 1996 New York Times #1 Best Seller book *Emotional Intelligence* that sold over 5 million copies worldwide in 40 languages, he suggested your emotional quotient (EQ) is more important than the traditional intelligence quotient (IQ) in determining your success in life. Dr. Goleman argues that the reason why people with high IQs can fail or flounder in life and people with modest IQs can be successful in life is because the successful person with the modest IQ has a higher emotional intelligence (EQ) than the unsuccessful person with the high IQ but lower EQ.

This argument by Dr. Goleman can also help explain the driving force behind the long list of successful and wealthy people in life without higher education degrees making millions of dollars; including people that are high school or college dropouts or without any college education at all. A **high EQ** that Dr. Goleman points out along with some **true grit** that Dr. Duckworth talks about is a winning combination for great success in life—especially in your job interview.

Focusing on developing one's EQ is not just for people seeking to impress hiring managers in job interviewers or current employees seeking to perform better at their jobs. Higher EQ levels also produces better leaders. In his international bestseller, *Primal Leadership: Unleashing The Power of Emotional Intelligence*, Dr. Goleman, along with co-authors Drs. Richard Boyatzis and Annie McKee, performed research on workplaces led by over 3,870 executives. After their research, they discovered that the most effective business leaders are those who understand and harness their emotional intelligence, not their IQ, in leading their people.

Like Dr. Bradberry and TalentSmart, Dr. Goleman and his colleagues teach that your emotional intelligence (EQ) involves malleable traits that can be learned, taught, changed, developed and managed. Rather than focusing on one's IQ in predicting a person's success in life, Goleman suggests people develop their EQ in order to increase their chances for a more successful life.

Clearly, understanding and developing your emotional intelligence (EQ) will help provide you greater success in your job interviews and career.

The Importance of Attitude in Your Job Interview

Attitude is all about how you carry yourself in the job interview. Your attitude, whether it's positive or negative, is affected by your thoughts, beliefs, emotions, feelings and opinions about someone or something.

A person with a positive, optimistic attitude sees themselves, their circumstances and their outlook on life through the lens of confident expectations of good, happiness and success regardless of the situation.

Just as a person with a positive attitude, it's important for you to be in the right frame of mind during your job interview. I understand you could think of 50 other places you'd rather be than in a job interview, but during your interview is not the time to let those negative feelings or thoughts about job interviews undermine the type of attitude you need to display in front of your hiring manager and other interviewers.

Don't walk through that doorway into the job interview room as if you are the character in the 14th century epic poem *Divine Comedy*, written by Dante Alighieri, who is walking through the vestibule of hell (Dante's Inferno) which bore the inscription over the doorway: "*Abandon all hope, ye who enter here.*"

You're not that poor slob in *Divine Comedy* who, in our context about job interviews, allegorically has to make his journey through the chambers of hell filled with interviewers carrying pitch forks; past the purgatory of a barrage of questions; until you finally make your way to the paradise of a new job. You are not Dante in the *Divine Comedy* and your job interview is not a punishment; it is an opportunity for you to move forward to something better in your life.

You want your hiring manager and other interviewers to see you as a person who has a positive attitude that they would enjoy working with; someone who is enthusiastic and excited about this job opportunity. Every workplace has its share of whiners, complainers and other types of people with negative, pessimistic attitudes that can pull people down at work. The last person your hiring manager and other interviewers want to hire is another person with that type of attitude.

The workplace is going to challenge you with many problems you'll have to solve. Employers want to know if you are the type of person who can face these challenges with a positive attitude that believes he or she can solve problems and produce good results.

So give yourself permission to breathe, relax, smile, and think happy, confident, positive thoughts while you're in your job interview. Learn to loosen up and enjoy the job interview experience. Don't be wound so tight that you can't think straight or laugh or respond correctly to humor.

One of my colleagues and I were newly hired for a large company. When he and I had a chance to talk about our recent job interview experience, he told me that after his job interview he immediately went out and bought five new suits for work. Apparently, his interviewers told him tongue-in-cheek that everyone wears suits five days a week at work. They expected him to take that statement lightheartedly, but instead, he took them seriously and spent some hefty cash for five new suits. On his first day of work, when he was the only one wearing a suit and tie while everyone else was in their business casual slacks and jeans; that's when he realized that they were just having fun with him. That's what can happen to you when you are wound too tight during your job interview. So relax; your interviewers are people too. They like to smile and joke with you too during your job interview.

As you move from junior to senior positions in your career, your hiring manager and interviewers are going to expect you to display more confidence in yourself along with a positive attitude as you move up in your career. Senior professionals are not only expected to show higher levels of knowledge and experience in a desired role, they are expected to show more leadership qualities which require confidence and a good attitude.

When you walk in that door to the job interview room, walk in there with your head held high, your shoulders back and your chest out like you own the place; like you're the most important person in the world.

Not with an arrogant air about you, but with a quiet confidence that says, "*I got this.*" Give yourself permission to feel good about yourself like you're king or queen for the day during your job interview. Walk in that job interview room with a *positive* attitude—you got this.

You are not at a disadvantage in the job interview; you are on equal footing with the hiring manager and other interviewers. After all, **they have just as big a need as you:** they need someone like you to fill a much-needed position in their workplace; and you need someone like them to provide you a job.

Think of it like this: your job interview with them is going to be either a win-win situation for both of you or a lose-lose situation for both of you; not a win-lose situation. If they hire you, both of you win by fulfilling both of your needs. You filled their need for another much-need person and they fulfill your need for a job. If they don't hire you, both sides lose in that situation. Both you and they have to continue the interviewing process; something both sides would rather end by you being the one they hire.

Did you get that? What I'm saying is the hiring manager wants YOU to be the one he or she hires because the hiring manager doesn't want to continue searching for and interviewing people to fill that empty position. Managers are busy people who would rather YOU were the one they hired than having to keep looking for someone else. Managers are responsible for the success of their team; and part of that success is making sure they have enough people on their team. The hiring manager wants YOU to succeed in your job interview because his or her team seriously needs YOU. Therefore, be that person with a positive attitude that makes the hiring manager's job easier in hiring you for the job.

A positive attitude not only helps you have a more successful career; a positive outlook on life is better for your overall health. The well-known Mayo Clinic is one of the world's best hospitals and ranked number 1 on the list of nearly 5,000 "Best Hospitals" on the 2014–2015 U.S. News & World Report. The Mayo Clinic staff posted an article titled *Positive thinking: Stop negative self-talk to reduce stress* that shows an optimistic or pessimistic attitude can affect your health and well-being.

The Mayo Clinic stated that the health benefits of positive thinking include, increased life span, lower rates of depression, lower levels of distress, greater resistance to the common cold, better psychological and physical well-being, reduced risk of death from cardiovascular disease, and better coping skills during hardships and times of stress.

Even King David understood the power of positive self-talk. King David faced many challenges in life, including having to face the giant Goliath in battle. The Psalms in the Bible that David wrote are filled with words of positive self-talk and encouragement to himself as shown in these following verses:

I have calmed and quieted my soul, like a weaned child with his mother; like a weaned child is my soul within me.

Psalm 131:2 NKJV

Why, my soul, are you downcast? Why so disturbed within me? Put your hope in God, for I will yet praise Him, my Savior and my God.

Psalm 43:5 NIV

Let all that I am wait quietly before God, for my hope is in Him. He alone is my rock and my salvation, my fortress where I will not be shaken. My victory and honor come from God alone. He is my refuge, a rock where no enemy can reach me.

Psalm 62:5–7 NLT

Power Posture, Power Thoughts, Power Words and Power Prayer for Job Interviews

Your attitude is also affected by your body posture, your thoughts and your own words while standing or sitting. Having the right posture—standing with your shoulders back and your chest out in a comfortable position or sitting upright or slightly forward in your chair—will not only make you feel more confident in yourself during your job interview; your hiring manager and other interviewers will notice your confidence and enthusiasm based on your posture too. It has long been proven that your posture affects your attitude and confidence just as your thoughts and words do.

How Posture Impacts Your Job Interview

In 2009, **Dr. Richard Petty**, Professor of Psychology at Ohio State University, and two other OSU alumni, Pablo Brinol and Benjamin Wagner, performed a research study of 71 students. In this study, students were asked to either sit upright with their shoulders back and their chest out or slouch in their chairs in front of a computer while they rated themselves as future professionals in a job. The results of the study, titled *Body posture effects on self-evaluation: A self-validation approach* was published in the February 2009 edition of the European Journal of Social Psychology.

This study found that students rated themselves more highly with confident, positive self-attitudes for jobs when they sat upright than when they slouched in their chairs. In other words, when the students sat in a position of power—upright—they felt empowered; therefore, they rated themselves highly. When they slouched in their chairs—a position of weakness, they felt less empowered; therefore, they rated themselves low.

In 2012, **Dr. Amy Cuddy**, a social psychologist working as an Associate Professor of Business Administration at Harvard Business School and author of the multi-best seller book, *Presence: Bringing Your Boldest Self to Your Biggest Challenges*, gave a TED talk on TED.com, a nonprofit organization that shares ideas about technology, entertainment and design (TED) worldwide. Dr. Cuddy gave her talk, titled *Your body language shapes who you are*, at TEDGlobal 2012 in Edinburgh, Scotland which has been viewed more than 33 million times on TED.com.

Dr. Cuddy shared how her research and experiments along with colleagues Dana Carney and Andy Yap of UC-Berkeley show you can fake confident body postures of dominance and power, something she calls **"power posing"**, for as little as two minutes, even when you don't feel confident, to increase testosterone levels in your body; decrease cortisol levels; and increase your desire for risk-taking which causes you to perform better in job interviews.

Dr. Cuddy's research states that power people and leaders—your alpha types—show significantly higher levels of testosterone and significantly lower levels of cortisol than the less powerful beta types.

Alpha types are people—male or female—who are more confident, extroverted, dominant, engaging, competitive, calm and non-reactive under pressure, assertive and charismatic than their beta counter-types. They also like standing out and speaking out in a crowd; and are risk takers because of their strong feelings of confidence and optimism, their desire to win in every situation and their lack of fear in failing.

Beta types—male or female—are more careful and less optimistic about things which make them less confident, vocal, outgoing, confrontational, engaging and assertive than alpha types. They're more passive, timid, shy, quiet, introverted and reserved than their alpha counter-types.

Cortisol is a natural steroid hormone in your body, also referred to as a "stress hormone" that increases your adrenalin to prepare your body for "fight-or-flight" situations. When your cortisol levels increase, your body becomes flooded with glucose; your arteries become narrow and your heart rate increases; making you feel more nervous and excited and less at ease during job interviews.

Dr. Cuddy's research shows that if you posture your body in a way that reflects dominance, power and confidence (the byproduct of alpha types), your brain and mind will also think the same way, triggering your body and emotions to follow suit. This will help give you more confidence and put you at ease and in a stronger frame of mind during job interviews.

What Dr. Cuddy recommends job-hunting candidates do before meeting the interviewers at their job interview is to spend at least two minutes in private, such as in a bathroom, an elevator, a vacant room or at home before they leave, standing in a "power position".

A standing power position is any alpha type standing position, such as standing with your shoulders back; your chest out; your head held looking straight ahead; your feet spread apart; and both hands resting confidently at your hips. Hold that position for at least two minutes to give your mind and body time to accept and adjust to that power position.

Dr. Cuddy is basically telling us to do with our bodies (power poses) what motivational speakers have been telling us for decades to do with our mind, thoughts, visualization and imagery techniques (power thoughts), and our words and vocalization (power words) to influence our self-talk in a positive way.

Dr. Cuddy's research on how power postures increase testosterone levels and decrease cortisol levels in your body may also lend a scientific explanation for why power thoughts and words taught by motivational speakers (such as Tony Robbins, Zig Ziglar and Jim Rohn) and by preachers of positive thinking (such as Norman Vincent Peale and Joel Osteen) actually work for so many people.

Whether we choose to listen to Dr. Cuddy or one of your favorite motivational speakers, mentors, life coaches or spiritual leaders; their end goal is the same: to help you become more confident, strong, positive, likeable and optimistic in your life, including in your job interviews.

How Power Thoughts and Power Words Impact Your Job Interview

Dr. Jim Taylor holds a Ph.D. in Psychology from the University of Colorado. He is a former Associate Professor in the School of Psychology at Nova University in Ft. Lauderdale and current adjunct professor at the University of San Francisco and the Wright Institute in Berkeley. Dr. Taylor has worked with professional and Olympic athletes in football, baseball, triathlon, golf, cycling, tennis, skiing and other sports. He's been a consultant to the US and Japanese Ski Teams, the US Tennis

Association, USA Triathlon; and was invited by Olympic committees of the US, Spain, France and Poland to speak to their athletes and coaches.

In a 2012 *Psychology Today* article, titled *Sport Imagery: Athletes' Most Powerful Mental Tool*, Dr. Taylor wrote, *"Imagery also isn't just a mental experience that occurs in your head, but rather impacts you in every way: psychologically, emotionally, physically, technically, and tactically. Think of mental imagery as weight lifting for the mind."*

Most of your top athletes and professional sports athletes use imagery techniques, also known as visualization, to rehearse their sport in their mind to maximize their sports performance. For example, football players will use sport imagery to visualize themselves catching the ball and running it in for a touchdown in the Super Bowl; baseball players visualize themselves hitting a homerun in the World Series; basketball players imagine themselves hitting 3-point shots in the NBA Finals; soccer players see themselves kicking the game-winning goal during the FIFA World Cup; and Olympians like Michael Phelps see themselves winning another gold medal while beating the living crap out of his South African rival swimmer, Chad Le Clos at the 2016 Rio Olympics. (I meant beating him in swimming.) These athletes are taught these imagery techniques to increase their positive self-talk and help them perform at higher levels when they are in competition.

After the Denver Broncos won the 2016 Super Bowl 50 Championship against the Carolina Panthers, Von Miller, the Super Bowl MVP, was surrounded by "Primetime" Deion Sanders and other NFL Network reporters. One of the reporters asked Miller if he ever saw himself where he's at now—at the Super Bowl level as the MVP. Von responded by saying, *"I do a lot of self-visualization and imagery . . . it was easy to say we're going to win the Super Bowl."*

Have you ever noticed how every time when the media asks a professional athlete how they feel about their upcoming championship game, they always respond the same way: *"It's just another game."*? In other words, these athletes are saying this all-important championship game is *no big deal.*

Their response is a visualization technique they've learned in order to make a very big event appear very small in their mind in order to control their emotions; stay focused and mentally tough; reduce their anxiety; and see their own selves as bigger than the championship game. They've trained themselves to make something very big look very small in their mind's eyes. Although they will prepare, train and practice as if it's the biggest event in their life; they train their minds with imagery and positive self-talk to think this game is just like any other regular season game.

You need to do the same thing for your job interviews. You should prepare as if each job interview is the biggest event in your life but you need make this important event appear very small in your mind to control your emotions; reduce your anxiety to help you relax; and make yourself feel bigger and more powerful than this job interview.

The reason you become nervous, fearful and anxious about job interviews, speaking in public or other similar life events are because of your *negative* imagery, visualization and self-talk about the situation.

Instead, you need to train yourself to think and see yourself in a *positive* light in these situations. Visualize and imagine yourself knocking that job interview out of the park. Imagine yourself being comfortable and confident in your job interview. Visualize yourself giving a great introduction and answering your technical/professional and cultural fit questions with great answers in your job interview. See yourself feeling and speaking confidently in your job interview. These visualization and imagery techniques will reinforce your positive self-talk and help give you the confidence and power to perform well in your actual job interview.

How Power Prayers Impact Your Job Interview

Of all the techniques you can and should use to encourage yourself, build yourself up, remove your fears and calm your nerves for your upcoming job interview, I believe there is nothing more powerful than simply praying about your next job interview. All of these other techniques I just shared with you will definitely help you strengthen your mind, your thoughts and your attitude. Prayer, on the other hand, helps to strengthen all of those things in addition to strengthening your spirit— that person deep down inside you we oftentimes call the "soul".

There is a God in heaven who hears all prayers; and He wants you to be more successful in life than you do. We may use our mouth or our mind or our body when we communicate with God, but that communication flows through our soul (our spirit) to God's Spirit. It's one thing to have yourself, family and friends in your corner on your side during your job interview. It's another thing to have Almighty God in your corner on your side during your job interview.

So ask God to help you with your job interview. He wants to help you. Ask God to help you prepare for your next job interview; to review the proper materials; and have everything ready to go on the day of your job interview. Ask God to remove all your fears, calm your nerves and give you the strength and courage you need to perform confidently, comfortably and successfully in your job interview. Ask God to keep your mind fresh and alert to be able to answer all the questions correctly that the hiring manager and other interviews might ask you. Ask God to give you favor in the eyes of the hiring manager so that he or she will select you for the job you want.

I always pray to God for His help when I'm preparing for my next job interview. Perhaps that's why I never experience any fear during job interviews. I enjoy every minute of the job interview process. Give it a try next time you have to prepare for your next job interview—you may be pleasantly surprised at the answers to your prayers!

Ask and it will be given to you; seek and you will find; knock and the door will be opened to you. For everyone who asks receives; the one who seeks finds; and to the one who knocks, the door will be opened.

Which of you if your son asks for bread, will give him a stone? Or if he asks for a fish, will give him a snake? If you, then, though you are evil, know how to give good gifts to your children, how much more will your Father in heaven give good gifts to those who ask him!

Matthew 7:7–11 NIV

Power Postures, Thoughts, Words & Prayer—Use It or Lose It

With this entire overwhelming evidence showing the advantages and benefits of power postures, power thoughts, power words and power prayers, why not make use of all of the advice given by these experts and the Bible?

The best part about these power poses, power thoughts, power words and power prayers are that they are all *free* just like the air you breathe; just take it in and breathe it out. I recommend you try using power thoughts and words from whichever motivational speaker or spiritual leader you choose along with Dr. Cuddy's 2-minute power pose, preferably in front of a full-length mirror if you have one available.

So try these power poses, thoughts, words and prayers several times hours or days before your job interview. Give yourself a healthy dose of these confidence boosting techniques before and during your job interviews.

As Dr. Cuddy said at the close of her TED talk, *"Don't fake it 'til you make it. Fake it 'til you become it."* Just ask the champ. Muhammad Ali said, *"To be a great champion, you must believe you are the best. If you're not, pretend you are."* Keep faking those power postures, power thoughts and power words and keep praying those prayers until they make sense to your mind, emotions, body and spirit and you become it.

Other Factors That Impact Your Job Interview

How the Chair You're Seated on Impacts Your Job Interview

The chair you're sitting on can also affect your posture in job interviews. I already shared with you Dr. Richard Petty's experiment with students that revealed the way you sit in a chair can affect the way you feel about yourself. If you sit in a position of power (sitting upright), you will feel more empowered and confident. If you slouch in your chair—a position of weakness, you will feel less empowered and confident.

When taking your seat in the job interview room, check the height of the chair to ensure it's at a comfortable height that allows you to sit upright. Go ahead and adjust the chair if you need to raise or lower it.

Oftentimes, interviewers will seat you on one of those swivel office chairs that allow you to adjust the height. The height adjuster is a metal lever underneath the right or left side of the seat. The chair lowers with your bodyweight when you pull up on the lever. To raise the seat, reach underneath the chair and pull the lever up with your fingers while rising up with your legs from your seat. The seat of the chair should rise on its own with you.

Some office swivel chairs will lean back when you sit in them. If your chair leans back, try to lock it in the upright position. If there is a lever underneath the chair to adjust the height, there should also be another lever underneath the chair that allows you to lock the chair in an upright position.

How Your Eye Contact and Head Impacts Your Job Interview

Two other areas that impact your job interview are your eye contact and your head level. Always maintain good eye contact when speaking with someone in the job interview room. Maintaining eye contact shows you are not only a confident person but also someone interested in what the hiring manager or other interviewers have to say. When you don't maintain good eye contact while having a conversation with someone, it makes you appear unsociable, disinterested, weak or as if you have something to hide.

The type of person you want to project during your job interview is a sociable, personable, confident person who is interested in what the hiring manager or other interviewers have to say; and someone who is enthusiastic about working on their team. Good eye contact communicates those things to the hiring manager and other interviewers.

Obviously, your head should move naturally along with your eyes in the direction of the person you are speaking with. Although you want to maintain a power posture when seated, you don't want to become stiff to the point that your eyes move but your head doesn't like a ventriloquist's dummy. Try to relax and allow your body movements to flow naturally with the person you are addressing. You can practice these things during role-playing job interviews.

Although your head should be allowed to move freely from side-to-side as you look at the person speaking in the job interview room, your head position should not be looking up toward the ceiling or down toward your hands, your watch or the floor. Looking up at the ceiling makes you look like you're lost in space or at a loss for words. Looking down makes you appear weak, a failure or loser, or as if you are lying. Looking down at your watch makes you look disinterested in being in your job interview and that you have somewhere else to go.

If the hiring manager or other interviewers ask you a question you don't know the answer to, don't start looking around the room in desperation, waiting for some epiphany to reveal the answer to you. Just look the interviewer in the eyes and say, *"I don't know the answer to that question."* Your straightforwardness and honesty make you look much better in the eyes of the hiring manager and other interviewers than that "deer in the headlights" look as you ponder the universe for the answer.

Where to Put Your Hands in Your Job Interview

Lastly, your hands and forearms should rest naturally on the desk in front of you. You can use your hands when you talk to emphasize a point, but don't wave your hands around constantly when you talk like a conductor of a symphony or something.

Never put your hands in your pockets while you are standing; don't hide your hands on your lap below the table in front of you; and don't put your hands in your pockets when seated during your job interview. Sorry if I sound like your mother taking you to your first day at school.

There may be occasions in a job interview where it would be acceptable to have your hand resting on your lap. For example, one job interview I went to took place in the hiring manager's small office. I sat on a swivel office chair in front of the manager's desk. The front side of the manager's desk was paneled so I could not place my legs under the desk. There were also four other interviewers in the manager's office to my left sitting in chairs against the wall.

In this scenario, I chose to keep the right side of my chair stationary up against the manager's desk while the front of my chair was facing the four interviewers sitting against the wall. I placed my right arm and hand on top of the front end of the manager's desk, and my left hand rested comfortably on my left lap. I could have also placed both hands on my laps if I wanted to in this scenario. My chair leaned back and it did not have an adjustment lever under the chair to lock it in place; however, I resisted the temptation to sit back in that chair. Instead, I sat upright in my chair the whole time.

I only had to turn my head to the right when talking with the hiring manager, and looked straight forward when talking with the four other interviewers who asked most of the questions. The hiring manager hired me for this job.

In another job interview I attended, the hiring manager and other interviewers wanted me to meet them at a local restaurant during happy hour. There were four of us that sat on bar stools around a small tall table with just enough room for finger food and beverages which the hiring manager ordered for all of us to enjoy while I was being interviewed by them. Except for the fact that I was wearing a suit and tie while they and everyone else at their tables around us were wearing their normal business casual, this was the ultimate relaxing job interview environment.

It was obvious the hiring manager and the other interviewers wanted to see how I would fare in a relaxed outing with them—my *cultural* fit on their team. However, this was still a job interview, so I maintained good posture sitting upright as best as I could on my bar stool and maintained eye contact when speaking with each of them. When they asked me a question, I looked them in the eye and did not look down or up when I answered their questions. We laughed and joked as well; and overall had an enjoyable time together during this job interview as we snacked on finger food and drank beverages. The best part was I got hired for that job too.

When you weigh all the mental (technical/professional fit) and social (cultural fit) factors that go into successfully completing a job interview; the truth is you need IQ, EQ and attitude in your job interview. However, don't assume hiring managers and interviewers are going to weigh IQ above your EQ and attitude. Naturally, you need to show the hiring manager you have the ability or capacity to learn, understand and apply information and skills by answering their technical/professional questions satisfactorily. You also need to demonstrate to the hiring manager that you have the ability or capacity to work well with other people, particularly people in your workplace and on your team, by your communications skills, personality, mannerisms and behavior—this is your EQ and attitude which translates to your cultural fit.

Job Interview Questions and Answers

The Interviewers Asking You Questions

After all the introductions are out of the way at the beginning of your job interview, the hiring manager and the other interviewers will begin asking you technical/professional questions. Depending on your profession, job interviews may consist of the hiring manager only or the hiring manager with 2–5 other people in the room as they ask you questions. Usually, all the people in the job interview room will take their turn asking you questions. Typically, the fewer interviewers there are in the room, the more questions each interviewer will ask you. The more interviewers there are, the fewer questions each will ask in order to stay within their scheduled job interview timeframes. It is also possible (although rare) for one of the interviewers who finished asking you questions to ask you a one or more questions later on during your job interview.

The hiring manager may or may not ask you technical/professional questions depending on the manager's knowledge and experience about the position they are trying to fill. I've been in a job interview with only two people—the hiring manager and the team lead. Both the hiring manager and the lead engineer asked me technical/professional questions in that job interview. I've also been in job interviews with only the hiring manager present who was asking me questions.

It is also possible that some of the interviewers present in the room won't ask you any questions. That may be the case when the interviewers have different career paths, but they are all on the same team.

Although the topics you see in the job description are the areas where the interviewers will focus their questions on; areas outside the scope of the job description are also open game for questions, including all areas that are listed in your resume.

Interacting with Interviewers in Your Job Interview

Don't be long-winded when giving your answers to the interviewer's questions. Keep your answers short and concise. Most questions can be answered in 30 seconds or less. With the exception of a few technical/professional questions or your introduction where you would take more time to talk about yourself; if you are going over 30 seconds when answering a question, chances are you are using too many words to answer the question or you are struggling to answer the question.

If you don't know the answer, maintain eye contact with the person asking the question, be direct and tell the person you don't know the answer to that question. If you know part of the answer, go ahead and share what you do know so that the hiring manager will at least give you partial credit for knowing portions of the subject. Your half answer may be more than what other candidates being interviewed can answer about that particular question.

Sometimes an interviewer will ask you a question that doesn't make sense to you. It's not that you don't know the answer; you just didn't understand the question. If you don't understand an interviewer's question, let the interviewer know you're not sure what they're asking you. The interviewer asking the question or another interviewer will try to rephrase the question without giving away the answer.

You should demonstrate good communications skills throughout your entire job interview. The way you communicate with each interviewer will give them a sampling of your soft skills, your emotional quotient (EQ) and your cultural fit with both their team and their company. Your communications skills in your job interview is an indication of how you will communicate with everyone else at work once you are hired.

Part of good communications is showing the hiring manager and other interviewers you are a good listener. When someone else is talking, don't interrupt them for any reason. Wait until the person is done talking before you inject a comment, answer or question into the conversation. Don't dominate the conversation. Let the hiring manager and other interviewers set the pace and focus of the conversation throughout your job interview.

Never speak negatively about any past jobs, managers, supervisors, leadership, co-workers or company policies in your job interview. Speaking negatively about past workplaces, assignments and people does not reflect negatively on them; it reflects negatively on *you*. It shows you lack the maturity and professionalism to keep those negative comments to yourself.

When asked why you left your last job, don't speak negatively about previous co-workers or managers. Even if those people or companies were the reasons you left those jobs. Try to put a positive spin on why you left those former companies. Show the hiring manager and other interviewers that you have the maturity and class to speak well of former employers and colleagues. Talk more in terms of looking for new opportunities, challenges or other ways to increase your knowledge and experience in your field of work as reasons for deciding to move on from those companies.

The hiring manager knows that one day you'll leave their company too. If you start griping about former workplaces or colleagues, the hiring manager knows it will be only a matter of time that you will be griping about them in the future too. No one wants to hire someone like that.

Sometimes the hiring manager or other interviewers will bait you to see if you'll say negative things about your previous boss, colleagues or employer by asking you cultural fit questions, such as *"Tell me about a difficult boss you had in the past and how you dealt with that"* or *"Tell me about a time you had to work with a difficult person on your team."* Don't take the bait and start throwing people under the bus and running over them forwards and backwards as if they were creatures from a zombie apocalypse. That's not what the hiring manager and other interviewers wanted to hear from you. Maintain your composure and share how you handled those conflicts in the workplace with confidence, maturity and professionalism.

How to Answer Questions about Salary in Your Job Interview

On rare occasions, one of the interviewers might ask you what is your desired compensation or salary expectation. In other words, how much you want to be paid for this job. As I mentioned earlier, it is taboo for you to bring up your salary or benefits during your job interview. Doing so implies you are more interested in the money and company benefits than in the job. This will most certainly reflect poorly on you in front of the hiring manager.

But what do you do when one of the interviewers, such as the hiring manager, brings up the topic of salary in your job interview?

Do you start negotiating your salary right there on the spot? Do you reveal or talk about what hourly rate or annual salary you already agreed to with your staffing agency recruiter? The answer to all of these questions is typically **no**. You should not discuss your desired salary or company benefits with the interviewers regardless if you previously agreed to a salary with a staffing agency recruiter. Do not reveal your specific hourly rate or annual salary to the interviewers that you negotiated with a staffing agency recruiter. This rule also applies if you are being interviewed over the phone.

First, let's take the case where you've already agreed to an hourly rate or annual salary with a staffing agency who got you this job interview. Once you established your desired compensation with the staffing agency recruiter, the recruiter sent your salary request along with your resume to the hiring manager. The fact that you're sitting in that job interview room means the hiring manager and that company's human resources department has agreed to pay your desired salary when you are selected for the job. The hiring manager would not have asked to interview you if their company could not afford you.

Hiring managers or other interviewers that ask you about your compensation under these circumstances are either inexperienced at best or unprofessional at worst. If the hiring manager wants to talk with you about your salary requirements, the hiring manager should do so in private; not with all the other interviewers listening in on that conversation. Usually, the interviewer who asks you about your desired salary in front of the other interviewers either doesn't know they're not supposed to ask that question about money in front of everyone or they don't care that you've already arranged your compensation through your recruiter. In either case, you should avoid discussing your desired salary with them.

The only person in the interview room who has the right to ask you about your desired compensation is the hiring manager because he or she is the one who will approve your salary in coordination with the HR department. The hiring manager knows what each person is making for their position on his or her team you will be joining when you are hired because the hiring manager approved everyone's salaries; and some of those team members are in that interview room with you. The rest of those interviewers in the room do not have the right to know what your desired compensation is **before** or **after** you are hired.

If it is someone other than the hiring manager asking you about your salary during your job interview, they are being nosy and out of line. They just want to know if you will be making more or less money than they are making when you are hired. If the hiring manager or team lead presiding over the job interview is professional and on top of things, he or she will intervene and not permit an interviewer to ask you any salary questions.

Those other interviewers in the room with you should not know what each other's salaries are; nor should they be permitted to know what you will make when you get hired. Problems oftentimes arise when company employees or contractors talk about their salaries amongst themselves. Someone is going to come out on the short end of that conversation and realize they are getting paid less for doing the same job as the other person.

The hiring manager should know better not to ask you your desired salary in front of the other interviewers because some of those people sitting across from you in the job interview room will become your co-workers when you are hired. Those interviewers are employees or contractors just like you. When you start working with them, they'll already know what you make because you shared your salary information with them in your job interview.

Bad things can come out of sharing your salary information with interviewers because interviewers have egos too. If you quote an hourly rate or annual salary that is more than what these interviewers negotiated for themselves, one or several of them might vote against hiring you because you—a newbie—would be making more money than they who have been working there longer than you. They'll try to get the hiring manager to hire someone who will be making less money than them. This will make it more difficult for the hiring manager to hire you even if he or she thinks you're the best person for the job.

Equally worse is these interviewers might not welcome you with open arms on their team, nor be as helpful as they might have been once you're hired because they know you are making more money than them. Sounds pretty unprofessional and you're right; it is unprofessional but that's the reality of job interviews conducted by company employees and contractors.

Then what should you do when asked about salary in the job interview?

You have to be tactful in deflecting the question. By ***deflecting*** I mean you need to simply move or direct the conversation about money from that interview room to your staffing agency. Kindly and respectfully tell the hiring manager or other interviewer that you've already agreed to a salary with your staffing agency, so there is no need to go over your salary. This should send a signal to the hiring manager and other interviewers that you do not want to discuss salary; and all the interviewers should get the message, back off the salary question and move on to the next topic.

If the interviewers don't get the message the first time, you can reword the deflection again by telling them you're satisfied with what your staffing agency or recruiter is offering you for the position; and should they (the hiring manager and HR) offer you the job; you are ready to start working for them.

On rare occasions, I've had interviewers ask me about my salary expectations in job interviews; and I always answered them the way I'm suggesting you answer them. It works for me every time.

However, if the interviewer continues to press you for an answer about your desired compensation, you should tell the interviewer that your recruiter would be happy to discuss your salary requirements with them; but you would rather not talk money or company benefits in your job interview because you're there to talk about the job. The good news is you already know they can afford you—that's the beauty of working through a staffing agency.

Don't be upset when hiring managers ask you about your salary. It's usually a sign the hiring manager is interested in hiring you and sometimes they just want to know if their company can afford you.

Let's consider another scenario where you didn't get the job interview through a staffing agency.

Suppose you got an invitation to the job interview as a result of submitting your resume on the company's online career website; and during your job interview, one of the interviewers pops the question about salary. You can't deflect the question to a staffing agency recruiter because you didn't go through one.

True, but you should still deflect the question for two reasons:

1. You don't want all the interviewers in the room with you to know your salary.

2. You have greater leverage to negotiate a higher salary after they decide to hire you.

First, job interviews rarely involve only one interviewer. Jobs where you may experience a one-on-one interview between you and the hiring manager only may occur in businesses such as retail or restaurants. For other types of companies, there may be between 3 to 6 people interviewing you in-person or over the phone for that open position.

With this many people in the interview, there's usually interviewers in that room who should not be privy to salary information of other workers in their company, including your salary. The hiring manager or team lead in that interview should understand this just as in the previous situation where you have a staffing agency recruiter representing you.

By sharing your salary requirements in this situation (you didn't go through a staffing agency), you again run the risk of facing the same challenges that come with revealing your salary with your future co-workers.

Secondly, you have greater leverage in negotiating your salary if you wait until after the hiring manager has decided to hire you than you would if you tried to negotiate your salary during your job interview. Once the hiring manager decides to hire you and the company's HR department sends you an offer letter, you now have greater leverage to negotiate a better salary than you did when you were in the job interview. Why? Because that offer letter means the hiring manager and the rest of the interview team want you above all the other job-seeking candidates they've interviewed. This gives you some leverage now in your response to the HR department concerning your salary.

If the salary in the offer letter is too low for your liking, you can reply with a counter-offer asking for more money. Yes, this is taking a risk. HR can either agree to match your counter-offer or refuse your counter-offer and choose not to hire you. That's the beauty of being a free agent—you control the risk and reward of your salary negotiation. If your counter-offer is not an outrageous amount of money above their original offer, the HR department is going to be more willing to pay you the higher amount you requested because you've already gone through their job interview vetting process and have the seal of approval from the hiring manager and the other interviewers that you are the right person for the job they are seeking to fill.

You are taking a greater risk by asking for that higher salary during your job interview—before the hiring manager decided to hire you—than you are asking for that higher salary after the hiring manager wants to hire you. If you try to ask for more money while the hiring manager is still interviewing other candidates for the job, the hiring manager may be more inclined to pick another candidate with a lower desired salary than you for the job.

The key to dealing with this salary question during your job interview is to try and deflect and postpone revealing your desired compensation until after the hiring manager decides to hire you. You do not want to find yourself haggling over your salary with the people who are interviewing you—the people deciding whether or not to hire you. You want to reserve your salary negotiations for the HR department with whom you can be a little more hardheaded without offending the hiring manager or other interviewers and negatively impacting their decision to hire you. Once the hiring manager decides to hire you, then you can talk money with greater assertiveness and leverage.

So let the hiring manager's HR department make the first move in making you an offer before you talk salary. You might even be pleasantly surprised to find the offer from HR is equal to or higher than the amount you wanted for the job.

So how do you deflect their salary question in this situation?

You should use the same strategy as when you are represented by a staffing agency recruiter: **deflect** the question by moving or directing the conversation about money from that interview room you are in to another time and place. In other words, kindly and respectfully tell the hiring manager that you would enjoy working with them, but you prefer to not talk about money until he or she has made a decision to hire you. Again, this should send a signal to the hiring manager and other interviewers that you do not want to discuss salary, and all the interviewers should get the message and move on to the next topic.

You could also throw in phrases such as, *"I'm willing to stay within the budget projected for this position"* or *"I'll accept any reasonable offer."* This should satisfy their curiosity as to whether or not they can afford you and, hopefully, not press you any further about your salary requirements.

Telling the hiring manager that you are willing to stay within budget does not mean you can't negotiate your salary with the HR department later on after the hiring manager selects you for the job. It just means you are willing to work things out with the HR department; and if the salary is too low for you, you can either give HR your counter-offer or walk away as a last strategy to get paid what you want.

If your resources allow you the opportunity to walk away from a low salary offer, let HR know that you mean business about your desired salary and will pass on this job opportunity if you are not paid what you want. HR already knows the hiring manager and his or her team members want you on their team, so they're going to think twice about denying your counter-offer. I've done this several times in the past and it has worked in my favor.

After I successfully completed a job interview, the hiring manager wanted to hire me. I was using a staffing agency recruiter who revealed to me the salary that the hiring manager wanted to pay me. I wanted to be paid more, so I gave my counter-offer to the recruiter to pass on to the hiring manager. I specifically told the recruiter to tell the hiring manager that if they did not want to pay me my desired salary, I did not want the job. This was a gutsy move but I was willing to take the risk in order to reap the reward of working for a higher salary. If the hiring manager decided to pass on me, I had enough resources to continue my job search elsewhere.

I didn't hear from the staffing agency recruiter for a week and thought the hiring manager decided to pass on my counter-offer. However, at the end of that week, the recruiter contacted me and told me the hiring manager agreed to pay me my desired compensation; and I started working for that company. The beautiful thing of it was that none of the other colleagues in my office knew how much money I was making for that job because I never talked salary with my interviewers who had now become my colleagues at work.

Lastly on this subject of being asked salary questions, if your personality does not hold up well under the pressure of the hiring manager or another interviewer asking you to talk about salary; and you feel compelled to discuss your salary; then do yourself a favor and start with a "salary range" instead of a "specific salary number". This way you give yourself a better chance of falling within the company's budgeted salary for that position. If you quote a specific salary number that is above what they are offering for the position, you stand the chance of losing out on being selected for the job altogether because the hiring manager knows they can't afford what you want or they can hire someone for a lot less.

Question on How Soon Can You Start Working

Oftentimes, at the end of a phone or in-person interview, I'm asked the question: *"How soon can you start?"* Obviously, this is a good sign when you are asked this question because it means the hiring manager is interested in hiring you. As tempting as it might be to belch out, *"Right now!"* don't do it. That answer makes you sound desperate more than excited or enthusiastic for the job.

If you are currently employed, tell the hiring manager that you need at least two weeks to give your current employer notice of your resignation. This will let the hiring manager know you are a person of integrity, respect, responsibility and fairness by doing the right thing in giving your current employer a two-week notice. The hiring manager and other interviewers know you will afford them the same courtesy when the time comes for you to leave their company too. This scores huge points in the emotional quotient (EQ) area of your "cultural fit" in the eyes of your interviewers.

If you are working through a staffing agency, let the hiring manager know you want the job but you also understand there is in-processing involved with the staffing agency before you can start work by saying, *"I'll need some time to get in-processed and on-boarded with my staffing agency, but as soon as that process is done, I'll be free to start."* The hiring manager will know exactly what you're talking about and will suggest a start date for you that allows you to first get on-boarded with your staffing agency.

If the job opening is a "direct hire" position (meaning you will be hired as an employee of the hiring manager's company instead of a "contractor" being paid by the staffing agency), the hiring manager will suggest to you a start date to show up for your first day of work.

If you need some time to take care of a few personal things before starting work, go ahead and tell the hiring manager you can start in a week or two weeks. If you need some extra weeks to move and relocate to your new employer's location, let the hiring manager know of your plans to relocate and the need for extra time for your move.

In one job interview, the hiring manager knew I would possibly have to relocate if he hired me because of the distance between my home and the job site. Therefore, he asked me what my plan was concerning my commute to work if I were hired. I told him I planned to move to their location. After the job interview, they hired me for the job; at which time I asked for three weeks to move to their location and get settled in which the hiring manager granted me.

Questions to Ask the Interviewers and Closure

More often than not at the end of your job interview, the hiring manager or another person leading the interview is going to ask you, "***Do you have any questions for us?***" Don't take lightly their invitation to you to ask them questions. You would be doing yourself a disservice if you pass on asking them any questions. Not asking any questions oftentimes shows your lack of preparation or lack of interest in the job or their company. This will cause you to miss out on another opportunity to stand out one last time above the other candidates being interviewing for this same job.

As I mentioned, the entire job interview process is about you making yourself stand out above all the other job-hunting candidates the hiring manager is going to interview; and this last part of your job interview should be used for that same goal. You should be ready to ask good, engaging *open-ended* questions that will require the hiring manager provide you more than just a yes or no answer.

Hopefully, you did your homework and researched the company; you read through the previous chapter on the do's and don'ts when you are asking the hiring manager your questions; and you prepared **2–3 questions** ahead of time. You can write or type out these questions and bring them with you to your job interview so that you remember to ask them at the end. I usually type these questions on my computer; print it out on one 8 by 11 inch sheet of paper; and then cut the sheet down to size to fit in my small portfolio I normally bring with me to job interviews.

Closing Statements at the End of Your Job Interview

After the hiring manager answers your last question, don't wait for the hiring manager to ask you if you have any closing statements because the hiring manager most likely will not ask you if you have any last words. Take the initiative to give the hiring manager and other interviewers your closing statements immediately after they've answered your last question.

In your final closing statements, there are two things you need to do:

1. Thank the interviewers.

2. Ask for the job.

Thank the Interviewers for Inviting You to the Job Interview

First, you should always thank the interviewers for taking time out of their busy schedules to interview you for this job. This lets the hiring manager and other interviewers know you get it; you understand that they have work to do but they're in that room with you to make this all about *you*—this is your job interview, not theirs.

Ask the Hiring Manager for the Job

Secondly, ask for the job. The greatest salesperson in the world will not make a single sale until they ask for the sale. The answer is always no until you ask for the sale. If you don't ask, you can't have. After everything the hiring manager has told you about the company; after all the questions they asked; let the hiring manager know you are still interested in the available position and you are still enthusiastic about working with them.

You could say something simple such as, *"I'd like to take this time to say thank you to all of you for taking time out of your busy day to interview me. I'm very interested in this job, and I would enjoy working with all of you on your team."*

Don't say, "***I want this job***", because those words make you appear desperate and it sounds like you just want the job and don't care about working with them.

Don't ask, "***When can I start?***", because that makes you come across as arrogant and as if you blindly presume you've already beat out all the competition before all the competition has had a chance to interview.

Can you take a more aggressive or assertive approach in asking the hiring manager for the job? Certainly, but I recommend doing so only if you sense that the hiring manager or other interviewers like you for either your **technical/professional fit** or **cultural fit** or both.

I went through a particularly grueling job interview where I was asked question after question by six interviewers who were there. They asked me a lot of questions that I didn't have the answers to. I was certain I was not the best technical/professional fit for that position but I was still very interested in the job and I wanted to work there.

Although I wasn't the smartest pea in the pod of candidates they would interview for this job, I could sense the interviewers enjoyed talking with me, and I felt I connected with them too. In other words, I knew I nailed it when it came to my emotional quotient (EQ) and cultural fit for the job.

So, in my closing statements, I asked for the job more aggressively by putting on a big smile, thanked them for interviewing me and told the hiring manager that I was very interested in the job and would love to work with each of them. Then I added with a smile, "***So what can I do to convince you guys to hire me?***"

The hiring manager responded, "***Give me a big sack of cash.***" (That tells you how poorly I performed with my technical/professional answers in the job interview.)

However, since I showed them my enthusiasm in wanting to work with them; and because we connected in common interests during our discussion that showed my cultural fit with them; they hired me for the job that I previously negotiated with my staffing agency recruiter.

That's the power of asking for the job.

PART THREE

AFTER THE JOB INTERVIEW

CHAPTER SEVEN

After the Interview—Now What?

There is a way to do it better...find it.
Thomas Edison

Congratulations!

You did it! You made it through your job interview—Congratulations!

In the closing scene of the animated movie *Finding Nemo* produced by Pixar, all the fish in the dentist's aquarium finally made their long-awaited escape after many failed attempts to break free from their watery prison in that dentist's office. They successfully turned their fish tank into a place that only Pigpen could love in a Charlie Brown special.

When the dentist placed all of the fish in separate plastic bags to clean the aquarium, each fish secretly rolled themselves to freedom out the open window like *American Ninja Warrior* contestants. They tumbled across the dangerous obstacles of a busy city street and hurled themselves over the water bank the way Olympic runners would throw themselves across the finishing line and basked in the ocean's winning circle like a racehorse that had just won the Kentucky Derby. As they bobbed together on the ocean's welcoming surface within their little plastic bags of freedom rejoicing over their victory; silence settles in among them.

Then one fish asks the all-important question: *"**Now what?**"*

That's sort of the way you feel after you completed your job interview. After jumping through so many hoops and making your way over so many obstacles to get to that all-important job interview; you did it and it's over. Now you're finally sitting there in silence, free again to contemplate what just took place. You made it out of the confines of that job interview room alive. You can breathe a great sigh of relief again like someone who was just let out of jail (or *Dante's Inferno*).

Like so many professional sports athletes waiting to find out if they made the team or if they're going to be cut, you're on the bubble waiting for what the future holds for you after completing your job interview.

You feel good about where you are now but you're still in this bubble, like those fish, asking yourself, "***Now what?***"

Here are a few things to consider while you wait to hear some feedback after a job interview:

- Sending thank you notes

- Perfecting your craft

- Other job opportunities

- The wait and the response

Sending Thank You Notes

Sending a thank you note to the hiring manager immediately after your job interview, thanking him or her for giving you the opportunity to interview for the job is still relevant advice today. It shows the hiring manager you do business in a professional and courteous manner. Using the thank you note is also a great opportunity to ask for the job again, as you did toward the end of your job interview; by letting the hiring manager know that you are excited about the opportunity to join his or her team.

If you plan to send the hiring manager a thank you note, try to send the note within 24 hours of completing your job interview. With today's technology, your thank you note can easily be sent via email to the hiring manager if you have access to the hiring manager's email address. Snail mail should be avoided due to postal delays that can occur internally and externally to the hiring manager's company.

With advances in technology and services come changes in the way people do business. This is also true with the thank you note after a job interview. When you are using a staffing agency, chances are you may not have access to the email address or phone number of the hiring manager. Why? Because the middle man—the staffing agency—is there to be a buffer between the employer and you.

Many hiring managers prefer to communicate with job-seeking candidates through the staffing agency; not directly with candidates. This gives the hiring manager the distance they oftentimes prefer to have between themselves and multiple job-hunting candidates interviewing for the job.

You can attempt to get the hiring manager's email address from your staffing agent, but don't be surprised if you are told the hiring manager prefers not to provide you their email or phone number before or after your job interview. Typically, what ends up happening is the staffing agency recruiter or account manager will provide you their own email address and phone number; and you will have to communicate with the hiring manager through the staffing agent.

Understanding how technology and staffing agency services have evolved, I don't bother trying to send thank you notes to hiring managers after my job interview if the staffing agent does not provide me the hiring manager's email address. This is an unwritten rule but acceptable practice when you do not have access to the hiring manager's contact information. If I'm provided the hiring manager's email address from the staffing agent, then I'll send the hiring manager a thank you note after the job interview.

Perfecting Your Craft

There's no better time to perform a self-evaluation on your job interview performance than right after you completed one. Ask yourself what you did well in the job interview and what you need to work on. Take this time to pat yourself on the back for the things you did well; and don't be so hard on yourself during your self-evaluation for the things you did wrong. You should be your greatest cheerleader whether your team is winning or losing the game.

Here are a few tips for perfecting your interviewing skills for your next job interview:

Tip #1: While your completed job interview is still fresh in your mind, try to write down every question that was asked of you whether you knew the answer or not. By writing down these questions, and finding the correct answers to them, you'll have a better barometer of how well you performed in your technical/professional fit and cultural fit for the job.

This will also give you valuable interview questions and answers that you can review for future job interviews. There's a good chance these same questions may be asked in future job interviews. The one thing that started me on the road to writing this book was my habit of writing down the questions I was asked during job interviews.

Tip #2: Go over in your mind how you presented your introduction to the hiring manager and other interviewers in your job interview. Were you cool, calm and collected? Did you remember everything you wanted to say in your introduction? Did you hit on all the right points that showed you were both a good technical/professional fit (based on the job description) as well as a good cultural fit (based on your social skills) to their company? Take notes of the things you could have done better so you can remember to incorporate those corrections in your preparation for future job interviews.

Tip #3: Evaluate how the effect of using role-playing, power poses, power thoughts, power words and power prayers helped your confidence level in your job interview. Did you remember to smile and maintain eye contact; hold your head up, shoulders back and chest out; and sit upright in a relaxed and comfortable manner? Were there other things you could have done to make yourself feel more comfortable and at ease in the job interview room? If so, make those adjustments in confidence boosting exercises for future job interviews.

Tip #4: How effective was your research on the company or interviewers? Did your research prove useful? Were you able to incorporate that information into the discussion, such as during your introduction? Did you strike a positive chord with any of your interviewers when talking about some of your personal interests, such as your hobbies, sports, volunteer work or other ways you spend your free time?

All of these things helped add to their perception of your cultural fit on their team and in their company. If any interviewers showed interest in your activities outside of work, you might want to consider using those same items in your next job interview to establish your cultural fit and rapport with your interviewers.

Other Job Opportunities

Just because you are scheduled for a job interview, that's no reason to discontinue or place on hold your job search activities with other staffing agency recruiters. I can't tell you how many times I thought the stars had aligned in my favor after completing a job interview; and I decided to forego pursuing any other job opportunities that staffing agency recruiters were offering me while I waited for the good news from the hiring manager that they wanted to hire me for the job. Then I realized those were shooting stars I was looking at because my hopes soon disappeared when I was notified that I was not selected for the job. By the time I tried to re-engage with those other staffing agency recruiters I had put off, those jobs had already been filled.

Note to self: Stop stargazing after the job interview is over and keep pursuing other job opportunities that are out there. Until you sign your offer letter for the job, nothing is concrete about the outcome of your job interview.

Keep your job search pipeline open for other job opportunities that come your way even if you are scheduled for a job interview or successfully completed a job interview. There's nothing illegal or unprofessional about checking other company websites for jobs or speaking with several staffing agency recruiters about different job opportunities at the same time. You can be sure both those staffing agency recruiters and company hiring managers are contacting and speaking with several job-seeking candidates at the same time, even if they currently have a scheduled job interview with you.

If things don't work in your favor after your job interview, hopefully you'll have several fallback job recruiters you can turn to immediately to continue your job search. The quickest way to get over the post-job interview blues is to be communicating with other staffing agency recruiters about other job opportunities.

If you are hired for the job after your successful job interview, you can proudly announce to the other staffing agency recruiters you were communicating with that you were hired for a job and are no longer on the job market.

The Wait and the Response

How long you have to wait to receive a response or feedback after completing your job interview depends on the hiring manager or the staffing agency's recruiter or account manager.

If the interviewing panel rated you as a potential fit for their team after your job interview; and they still have other candidates to interview, the hiring manager will wait until his interview panel has completed all other interviews before making a decision on which candidate is the best fit for their team. This process could take 1–3 weeks depending on how many candidates are being interviewed and where you are in the job interview pecking order.

After all candidates are interviewed, the hiring manager will let your staffing agency recruiter or account manager know if they selected you or not. If you did not use a staffing agency and worked directly with the employer's HR department, the HR rep will email or call you to inform you of either the good news that you were selected for the job or the bad news that you were passed over by the hiring manager.

What Happens If the Answer is No

If the hiring manager decides to pass over you after your job interview, the hiring manager will provide this feedback immediately to the staffing agency recruiter or account manager that set up your job interview with them. The hiring manager will not wait until all interviews are completed to pass along this bad news to the staffing agency. The manager will let the staffing agency do the dirty work of informing you that you were not selected. If your job interview was set up through the employer's HR department instead of through a staffing agency, the HR rep will let you know that you were not selected for this job.

Whether the results about your job interview turn out positive or negative, always show some class and be a professional by thanking the people who made your job interview possible—your staffing agents and the hiring manager. If the staffing agent is giving you the news over the phone, thank them there on the spot over the phone; otherwise a simple thank you in an email to the staffing agent will suffice. As previously mentioned in the section on sending a thank you note, you may not have access to the hiring manager's email address. In this case, there's no need contact the hiring manager.

Oftentimes, some staffing agencies will not contact you after the hiring manager has informed them that they did not select you for the job. Their lack of courtesy in notifying you has earned them the name of "head hunters".

You have two options when you've waited long enough for feedback about your completed job interview:

1.   The first option is to reach out to your staffing agent for status.

2. The second option is to accept the staffing agent's silence as meaning the hiring manager has not selected you for the job.

The first option is the best option because there could be multiple unplanned reasons that could delay a response back to you. There could be an unexpected number of job-seeking candidates submitted from various recruiters that the hiring manager wants to interview. The hiring manager or other key members of the interview panel may be out of office for personal or business reasons; therefore, they're waiting for that person to return. One or more pressing company issues or priorities may have placed the job interview process on hold. The company may be undergoing critical changes, such as management, hiring manager or organizational changes, which require the dust to settle on this internal transition before they can refocus on the job interview process again.

I've contacted staffing agents for feedback after a week or two of waiting, and oftentimes they've told me the delay was due to the reasons I just mentioned. So be easy on the recruiter. Don't pester the staffing agent or the hiring manager with multiple inquiries each week. Just one inquiry is needed. Maintain a courteous and professional attitude throughout this waiting period.

The second option is to accept the staffing agent's silence as meaning the hiring manager has not selected you for the job. I've used this option when I know I absolutely bombed my job interview. Under these circumstances, if I chose to contact the staffing agent, it would only be to confirm what the staffing agent and I already knew—I was not selected for the job.

Regardless of the choice you make to get some feedback about your job interview results; if it ends up being you were not selected for the job, move on and continue your job search with other staffing agents. Has this happened to me after a job interview? Yes, it's all part of the job search process.

How to Handle Rejection after a Job Interview

Rejection is a normal part of the job search process just as in other areas of life. Everyone has to go through rejection in one form or another, from candidates running for the US presidential office to candidates in search of work in the most menial of jobs. Don't let the rejection from an unsuccessful job interview hamstring or derail your momentum, enthusiasm, progress and success in your job search or job interview process. That closed door just means your job is still out there waiting for you to find it. Alexander Graham Bell said, *"When one door closes, another opens. But we often look so long and so regretfully upon the closed door that we do not see the one which has opened for us."*

Some people have a hard time with rejection. It makes them feel like a failure. They mistakenly identify an event with who they are as a person. It's not your failures that define you; it's how you respond to failures that matters. Failures refine you; they don't define who you are. You are not a failure just because you didn't get selected after a job interview. You are a successful person who experienced a failure. There's a difference.

Accept failures in life as a good teacher; the way you would accept the scores and remarks your teachers gave you on your papers in school. They are there to help improve your skills in life. Learn from failures the way you would learn from a coach telling you what you're doing wrong so you can improve your skills and performance to do better next time. They are there to make you a success, a winner, a champion in life. Embrace failures the way you did when you first embraced learning to ride a bike or skates or skateboard or snowboard or skis. Falling was all part of the process to rising higher. It is part of the adventure, the risk, the excitement and the fun of learning how to do something well in life. Sure, there will be some bumps and bruises along the way when you fall, but when you get back up and move on with your life, you become stronger, better and wiser for having gone through those falls.

Both players and coaches in professional sports know this mentor, teacher and life coach called *failure* all too well. Each year, these professional athletes and coaches fail to win games and are rejected, traded or fired from teams only to find themselves being hired again by another team, performing better and winning games another year. That's what failure produces—**SUCCESS**!

Failure is the secret ingredient to the recipe of success

As you prepare to move from one job to the next, one job interview to the next; remember, everyone falls every now and then. Every great champion has experienced failure and defeat. The key to success is getting back up and trying again.

LeBron James has won three NBA championships; received four NBA MVP Awards, three NBA Finals MVP Awards, two Olympic gold medals; in addition to being selected to 12 NBA All-Star teams, 12 All-NBA teams and six All-Defensive teams. In 2016, LeBron was the key reason the Cleveland Cavaliers won their first NBA Finals championship in franchise history. So, what's LeBron's view on failure? He said, *"You have to be able to accept failure to get better . . . You can't be afraid to fail. It's the only way you succeed—you're not gonna succeed all the time, and I know that."*

Michael Jordan led the Chicago Bulls to two separate NBA championship "three-peats" in 1991, 1992, 1993 and again in 1996, 1997, 1998 after coming out of a two-year retirement in 1993 and 1994. He set an NBA record with 72 regular-season wins in the 1995-96 NBA season. Jordan said, *"I've missed more than 9,000 shots in my career. I've lost almost 300 games. Twenty-six times, I've been trusted to take the game winning shot and missed. I've failed over and over and over again in my life. And that is why I succeed . . . I can accept failure, everyone fails at something. But I can't accept not trying."*

J. K. Rowling is the British novelist best known for writing the *Harry Potter* fantasy series whose writings became blockbuster films and theme parks. Rowling said, *"It is impossible to live without failing at something, unless you live so cautiously that you might as well not have lived at all, in which case you have failed by default."*

Steve Jobs was co-founder and CEO of Apple, CEO of Pixar Animation Studios and NeXT Inc., and on the board of directors of The Walt Disney Company. He was fired from Apple in 1985. Afterward, he founded the company NeXT and helped in the creation of Pixar that produced the first fully computer-animated film, *Toy Story*. Concerning his being fired by Apple, Steve Jobs responded with these words: *"I didn't see it then, but it turned out that getting fired from Apple was the best thing that could have ever happened to me. The heaviness of being successful was replaced by the lightness of being a beginner again, less sure about everything. It freed me to enter one of the most creative periods of my life."*

If you failed one of your job interviews; were passed over by the hiring manager for another candidate; consider yourself in good company. People greater than you have fallen a lot farther and harder than you; but they got back up and tried again.

That's what made them great!

That's what made them successful!

That's what made them a champion!

Let your failures teach you; let them refine you; let them improve you; but never let them stop you. Now get back up and try again. There is greatness in you. You are destined for success. **You're a champion!**

Straight from My Heart

It is my sincere hope that this book has blessed you, inspired you, strengthened and encouraged you in your job interview process. I gain no greater satisfaction in life than to pass along to others the things I've learned in life to help people live a successful, healthy and prosperous life—not just in this life but the next. What do I mean by the *next life*?

The last and most important interview questions: I'm not saying this will happen anytime soon, but if you were to die today, where would you go? If God were to ask you why should He let you into heaven, what would you say?

Here's your answer: The Bible says in Romans 3:23, *"All have sinned and fall short of the glory of God."* Romans 6:23 says, *"The wages of sin is death, but the gift of God is eternal life in Christ Jesus our Lord."* Romans 10:9 says, *"If you declare with your mouth 'Jesus is Lord,' and believe in your heart that God raised Him from the dead, you will be saved."* Romans 10:13 says, *"Everyone who calls on the name of the Lord Jesus will be saved."*

Pray this quick prayer with me: *Heavenly Father, I believe Jesus died on the cross for me and my sins, and rose again from the dead. I give You my life. Lord Jesus, come into my heart and into my life. Amen.*

If you prayed that prayer, you are saved and going to heaven when you die because Jesus paid for all your sins—past, present and future. That's the answer to your final and most important interview question you'll have in life.

Did you like *The Ultimate Job Interview Guidebook*? Did this book help you? If this book helped you, inspired you and gave you better insight and understanding of the overall job interview process, **tell your connected friends about this book on social media.** It's a great way to let your friends know about a great book that will help both you and them; and your friends will thank you for it. Let me be one of the first to say *THANK YOU* for introducing your friends to a book that will change their careers and their lives for the better.

Frank McClain

Also By Frank McClain

Book of the Year award winner *The Ultimate Job Hunting Guidebook*, award-winning *YOU'RE HIRED!* and *The Ultimate Job Hunting Guidebook for Military Veterans*

  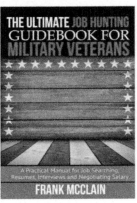

IT Questions & Answers For IT Job Interviews, Volume 1
IT Questions & Answers For IT Job Interviews, Volume 2
IT Questions & Answers For IT Job Interviews, Volume 3
IT Questions & Answers For IT Job Interviews, Volume 4
IT Questions & Answers For IT Job Interviews, Volume 5
IT Questions & Answers For IT Job Interviews, Volume 6

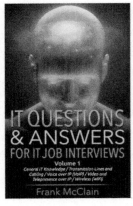

About The Author

Frank McClain is a multi-award-winning author who graduated with a BS in Information Systems Management from the University of Maryland. He is a military veteran who served 20 years in the US Air Force both in the US and Europe. He lived and worked in Europe for over 12 years both as a US military member and as a civilian government contractor. He's worked over 15 years as an IT consultant in both US government and corporate jobs in the US and Europe. Frank has extensive experience dealing with the job search process, job recruiters, job interviews and working for many Fortune 500 companies and US government agencies, such as the North American Aerospace Defense Command (NORAD), Missile Defense Agency (MDA) and the Defense Information Systems Agency (DISA). Frank currently resides in Colorado.

Printed in Great Britain
by Amazon

26525514R00099